The One Success Habit

You Can't Do Without

Dr. Fred Ray Lybrand

KAUFFMAN
BURGESS
PRESS

Fred Ray's done it again. He's masterfully taken a critical life-skill, the habits we harbor, and shown us how to practically make it come alive. His insight about actions and habits is simply brilliant.

–Mark Wasserman, Operator, Chick-fil-A Medical Center

Fred Ray Lybrand is an excellent communicator. His ability to present even complex concepts and topics in a clear and concise manner is extremely beneficial. He ties humor and his unique perspective together with real life examples to clearly relate his point. Dr. Lybrand's ability to understand a problem and identify the underlying factors causing it enables him to overcome the usual confusion and present a lasting solution. His clarity of thought and his conversational style creates the "a-ha" moment for the learner; who can immediately see a clearer path to success. I wholeheartedly recommend listening to anything Dr. Lybrand is explaining.

-Brad McMurray, San Antonio Housing Authority

Fred Ray Lybrand has the unique ability to lay the facts and observations of a situation out there without personal judgment and bias. He leaves you with the clear decision points that will take you further. However, be ready --- he'll leave you with a pretty clear idea of the choices before you, which then become pretty hard to ignore.

–Craig McCurley, P.E., JACOBS Global Buildings * Director, Central/South Texas Design Operations-

I've taught time management concepts for years, but Dr. Lybrand demonstrates a genius for simplifying and distilling key concepts for practical application. This book is a "must read" for everyone who really wants to get the most important things done! Witty, engaging, powerful, and effective -- also a quick read. You will get more done and experience less frustration each day if you read this book!

-Col. Brian Norman, International Consultant and former commander of the Air Force Manpower Agency, USAF, Retired

-Every organization participates in the practice of goal setting. It's how we move the needle forward. The challenge is that the processes used to determine our goals vary as widely as the goals themselves. Every time a new goal is set, a new result is achieved; that result either moves the organization forward, backward, or nowhere at all. In The One Success Habit (You Can't Do Without) Dr. Lybrand crafts a simple solution to inefficient day-to-day efforts that is applicable to any organization. If you are looking for a way to move your organization (or yourself) to the next level, or you just want to get un-stuck--- the solution is here.

-Nathan Pattison
Agency Field Consultant, State Farm Insurance

Fred Ray Lybrand has a gift for figuring out how life works through a balance of wisdom and intellect. He captivates diverse groups of people with his passion for telling the truth and his use of humor and wit.

- John Sanchez, CEO of Silver Creek Oil & Gas, LLC

To Tripp, Laura, Forrest, Holmes, & Brooks:

Behold, children are a heritage from the Lord, the fruit of the womb a reward. Like arrows in the hand of a warrior are the children of one's youth. Blessed is the man who fills his quiver with them.

-King Solomon

Look carefully then how you walk, not as unwise but as wise, making the best use of the time, because the days are evil.

–Saul of Tarsus, circa 62 A.D.

CONTENTS

The writer does the most who gives his reader the most knowledge and takes from him the least time.

–Sydney Smith

Introduction

I know you are reading this book because you think there might be an answer here.

Quite frankly, I think there is an answer; but, please hold it lightly. THE book on business success a decade plus ago was *Good to Great*, by Collins and Porras. It is still a popular book and was built on the best research methodologies with the insights of sharp minds. The book looked at companies that had been successful for a long time. In the final analysis 11 companies stood supreme:

- Abbott Laboratories
- Circuit City
- Fannie Mae
- Gillette
- Kimberly-Clark
- Kroger
- Nucor
- Philip Morris
- Pitney Bowes
- Walgreens
- Wells Fargo

We don't need to analyze them all to see the glaring fact that two of them (Circuit City and Fannie Mae) are no longer examples to follow. Circuit City no longer exists after bankruptcy, and Fannie Mae shares plenty of the blame for the economic problems surrounding the US economy beginning around 2008.

Frankly, the others probably shouldn't be counted on as having a corner on 'success' in business either. I only mention this to share with you the truth that there is no answer. All the research in the world won't really tell you much of anything. Fads come and go, and it's not that they are evil or aren't honestly successful in some sense---but Fads just don't stand the test of time. Please be wary on your quest to success. Bouncing from one faddish idea to the next will not likely get you where you want to go. Honestly, it comes down to a choice. You can pursue the Physics of Life (how it works) or the Fads of Life (what's in fashion for now).

Instead of a fad, you are about to encounter a principle. Principles are transferable, which means they can be applied in many settings across the boundaries of time and culture. A principle can be used in unique ways over and over again. Being principle-focused is essentially the same as being wisdom-focused. You will benefit greatly to go to www.onesuccesshabit.com to get your free copy of the workbook that accompanies *The One Success Habit*. It offers you a focused way to start establishing this life-changing habit deep into your soul.

There is no reason to believe me, though I can make many appeals to witnesses and anecdotes. When it gets down to it you will either try to build *The One Success Habit* into your life or you won't. If you try to build the habit into your life, then it will either work or it won't. That's all there is to it.

You see, most of us spend our lifetimes guessing about things and trying to make sense of them. Often we can get close, but the universe is loaded with mysteries.

So, you can (1) either learn a few principles and put the odds in your favor, or you can (2) keep trying to figure everything out before you take a single step and put your hope in luck (i.e., you'll be lucky if you have enough time left once you've made sense of everything).

Isn't it true that apart from areas of true faith we all finally rest on evidence and logic? Even your 'feelings' are a kind of evidence if you have learned to follow them because they are usually right. Logic is just what makes sense, but it is tricky too. It made sense to think stomach ulcers were caused by stress because a person with an ulcer was very stressed out. Yet, it turns out it is a bacterium that causes most ulcers. It made sense to blame stress, but only if you started with the wrong assumption.

Personally, I hold both logic and evidence lightly because I simply could be wrong. On the other hand, I'm not inactive because inaction all-but-guarantees failure. I suppose on some level it's best to notice that success and faith are a bit intertwined. The principle you are about to learn can change everything. It will feel right and it will make sense; yet, you won't make use of it unless you ask and answer a very strategic question...

Chapter 1

What is Success to You?

A few years ago 'de-motivator' posters became all the rage. The idea was to send a message while offering a dark kind of comfort. Here are a couple of my favorite captions as best my memory serves;

❖ *If at first you don't succeed…maybe failure is your thing*

❖ *Perhaps your life is just to serve as a warning to others*

The first had a dejected baseball player sitting on the bench, and the second had a half-sunken barge in the middle of the ocean. Almost immediately we all get the importance of success, but think a little deeper…

Why Does Success Matter?

On the surface, success matters because failure is so bad.

It does seem that most people operate with this kind of thought in the back of their minds somewhere. You know, it's simple. If you don't have money, friends, a lover, and stuff...life will be awful. Then again, I've worked with people over the years who fret over their money, are frustrated with their friends, want to get away from their lover, and are pretty bored with their stuff. In this kind of circumstance we find the first key to succeeding. Success is always relative. Success is always a 'compared to what' phenomenon. Success is driven by, and dies by, comparison. Are you a success? According to whom or according to what standard?

Honestly it just gets down to definitions.

Toward a Definition of Success

Clear definitions can solve all kinds of problems, especially conflicts.

> *Just definitions either prevent or put an end to disputes.* -Emmons

Isn't that true? Haven't you seen an argument suddenly stop because someone said, "Oh, I thought you meant..." The debate was in full motion because the facts were not clear.

Now think about success. What is your definition of success? How will you know when you get there? On any particular project or subject matter, how can you know a single step to take unless you've defined what success for that thing will be?

It isn't just for 'big picture' things either. The definition of success can matter for any item. How much money do you need to be a success? How much money do you need to be able to give away to be a success? Does it matter if the money is on paper, or do you need to be able to get to it? Change it to family---What does it mean to be a successful father, mother, or child? Is your children's success a part of your definition of success? If they fail do you also fail?

Most of the time we have not done the most basic of things---we have not defined our terms. Here are a few ways to ask the question for your own benefit.

> **What does success mean to me?**
> **When will I know I'm a success?**
> **How will I know I am a success at home, the office, in friendships, in love, etc.?**
> **Is there an area I have already succeeded in that I can learn from? What was my definition of success?**

It is high-time you define success in order to know what you are doing and why you are doing it. If you fail to sit down and clarify your own definition of what it means to be a success, then you have no real way to organize your actions or know when you've arrived. That may be the reason you have never defined it…if you don't define success, then you can never fail. Quite a strategy you have there, but there is one problem: Just because you never fail, it doesn't mean you have succeeded! Having no enemies doesn't mean you have lots of friends. You can still just be alone.

Thoreau's point that most people die with the 'song still in them' comes to the essential point of definition. If you haven't admitted you want to sing a song, or haven't admitted that the song is a ballad---well, then the song will stay inside till you die. If you won't start working on your definition of success, then quit reading this book and throw away your library on the subject. Nothing happens without a definition.

In many ways definition is more useful than vision. Defining a successful outcome of a meeting, a project, a business, or a life, can take care of the vision issue. Honestly, isn't a definition of a successful outcome the real vision you need?

My Definition of Success

It seems only fair for me to give you my own definition of success.

Frankly, this definition is a composite of elements I've found to be crucial through the years. Parts may be plagiarized, but it isn't intentional. In the history of the literature and the years of reflective reading, some of these things get so often quoted we think they are original with ourselves. If you show me who said what (from Epictetus to Napoleon Hill to Billy Graham), I'll be glad to note the reference. In the meantime, here's how I frame the word SUCCESS:

> **Success is achieving what is meaningful to me through the use of my best talents; without violating the rights or freedom of others and without offending God.**

Well, there is a lot here, so allow me to make a few comments on each part as it might relate to you.

- **Achieving what is meaningful to me** – Essentially this is about getting what you genuinely want or desire, but it considers how meaningful the accomplishment is to you as an individual. When you create a result that you want you are basically successful. Yet, we often don't feel it because it wasn't meaningful to begin with. The starting place is to let go of what everyone else is demanding (or you imagine they are demanding) in order to learn to be true to yourself. If it isn't meaningful to you, then why create it?
- **Through the use of my best talents** – Maybe you can create the results you want through your lesser talents, but I wouldn't bet on you. 'Nature'

has certainly designed you for something, or given you capacities to use in particular ways. These capacities need development in order to become skills. It is your love for the activity that allows the 10,000 hours you will invest to become a true master. Yet, even starting out, you are better than most people at certain things without much practice. These areas are where your talents live…and on balance, they are the means through which you will succeed.

- **Without violating the rights or freedom of others** – If you destroy people (or their property) on the way to success, you are still a big fat failure. Sorry for the moralizing, but that's the way it goes. What goes around comes around. You will reap as you sow. The Golden Rule is true. Attempting to manipulate and control others is tantamount to lying and cheating, which on any plane is failure. The reason manipulation amounts to cheating is that you are effectively removing the other person's choice when you manipulate…unless she can say, "No," then her answer is never a legitimate, "Yes."

- **Without offending God** – Now, this is clearly added because it is unique to me and my life orientation. If you are an atheist, scratch this part. Then again, if you are an atheist you don't think you can offend God since He doesn't exist--- so, you might as well leave it in! For the rest of us who believe in a Creator who is sovereign over all of His creation, it seems wise to take into consideration His standards. This doesn't have to be a set of rules, but it does mean that at least on the level of conscience we would be wise to stay decent in His eyes.

Well, there's my definition and you are welcome to borrow it, amend it, or toss it as you see fit. The reason I wrote it down was to create a context for my succeeding. What I pursue and how I feel about it really makes sense with this definition. The definition also helps me consider (or reject) possibilities that come my way.

Your Definition of Success

How about you? What is your definition of success?
Why not take a moment and write down something on a scrap of paper? If you don't define success, how will you know if you ever make it? How will you know if the steps you are pursuing will get you to what you really want in succeeding?

Pardon the illustration, but I remember asking my father, "When did you first realize you were a man?" He thought for a moment and said, "It was when I went home from college and smoked in front of my parents." Even as I write this I want to stress that I loved my dad and learned a mountain of valuable insights from him. However, on the definition of being 'a man', that's about as silly as it comes. It certainly never organized his life like a better definition might have, and it certainly didn't give me what I needed as to direction. My 4 sons all memorized a definition I heard from Robert Lewis during a trip to Little Rock. "A man is one who rejects passivity, accepts responsibility, leads courageously, and looks for the greater reward."

It has been a joy to watch my sons all check, challenge, and cheer for one another as they've grown toward manhood. Definitions can make a huge difference.

Don't underestimate the importance of working out your own definition of success; it will guide you toward wherever it points. Choose carefully, but choose now and improve it tomorrow.

The Need of the Moment

The need of the moment is for you to get started on a definition of success.

In a writing course (see it at **www.advanced-writing-resources.com**) I developed to help others overcome the same crippling fear of writing I had, I explain that writing occurs in **three stages**:

1. OK
2. Get Help
3. Make It Great

The idea is simply that most of us try to write something great from the moment we find pen and paper. The truth is that you can't start with perfect.

You can start with OK, however. Honestly, can you write an "OK" definition of success? Your definition of success should be nothing fancy and nothing to publish; just something OK.

Can you write that kind of a definition? Of course you can, and then you can get help with it. Show it to a trusted friend or two and see what they would add or take away. Play with it over a few days or weeks. Read it aloud and see what you think. Your definition can be a living thing and may take new shapes over the years. Nonetheless, your definition will give you a starting place.

Of course, it would be easier just to copy my definition down on a 3x5 card and reflect on it. I may have already saved you the time and hassle. Regardless, please make sure it is your own definition because you 'own' it.

Now, having a great definition of success is still meaningless unless you finally embrace one thing...

Chapter 2

So, Here's the Thing

It's probably a 'dirty little secret' or an 'insider's guide', but there is a simple and unexplored aspect to all self-help and positive thinking literature. The plain fact of the matter is that anything that gets someone to take action is going to produce some kind of result when compared to inaction. Did you get that? If you take action, your odds of success go up dramatically. This isn't rocket science (it isn't even calculus); the truth is simply that those who take action will almost always succeed over those who take no action. Even winning the lottery comes down to buying a ticket, though on very rare occasions a winning ticket is given as a gift.

Maybe it is positive thinking or maybe it is proving your high school classmates wrong; but all self-help and motivational efforts are focused on action. Let's face it--- **Action's the Thing!**

The True Lesson of the Tortoise and the Hare

Most of us know the age-old instruction from the race between the tortoise and the hare.

The stage is set between a boastful-yet-speedy hare and a humble-but-persistent tortoise. The big race begins and the rabbit gets so far ahead that he decides to take a nap. During the nap the underdog makes his way past the dozing foe to go on and win the race. Aesop's Moral: *Slow and Steady Wins the Race.*

On the surface this confirms our point that action is the thing. Just look at the story. The tortoise kept acting and the rabbit stopped acting. However, underneath the surface there is a point with a razor's edge. In what universe besides a fable does a tortoise beat a rabbit in a footrace? Statistically speaking, how many of these races if repeated over a period of years would the tortoise actually win? It seems likely that the right answer is, "Never!" Rabbits don't fall asleep while running and tortoises aren't racing animals (but it's only a fable). If we named it right it would be called "The Stupid Tortoise and the Narcoleptic Hare."

Here's the lesson: *Even though a rabbit can always beat a tortoise in a footrace,* **a tortoise that acts will beat a hare that sleeps.**

Of course, all fables are really about us. You know you have some kind of talent or knack that comes easier to you than almost anyone you've met. You don't need a test and you don't need an epiphany, you just need a little honesty about the matter. A good friend can be a big help seeing your unique ability.

There is something that comes as easy to you as running does to a rabbit. Moreover, you can even be paid to use it. Yet, you sleep...or research...or save...or worry...or talk about it...just a little more. It's all the same because **Action's the Thing**. The *One Success Habit* is all about action and exactly what must change for you to begin acting. In a sense, it is all about being a rabbit that finally wakes up in time to win the race.

The Goal of All Goals

In learning to appreciate that **Action's the Thing**, it is important to realize that action itself is the goal of all goals. A goal is simply an end result that you want to see happen. A goal can be a fine meal, an original work of art, or improved sales for a product. A goal is simply what you are aiming at, although we can call it a target, objective, creation, event, result, or outcome.

Oddly enough, we get confused on occasion because we really aren't clear about our real goal. Sometimes we think a by-product is the goal. By-products are great, but they are normally something we hope will happen as a result of reaching our goal. For example, your goal could be to write a book about something that is important to you. Your hope is that it might be a best seller. Being a best seller would be a by-product. Of course, being a best seller might really be your goal (which would dictate the kind of book to write); in which case winning a Pulitzer Prize would be a hope or by-product. It doesn't matter what your goal is, you can always have hoped for by-products.

The reason we need to understand the relationship between goals and by-products is that our actions are determined by where our focus rests. Writing a book about something important to you will invite you to take one path, while writing a Pulitzer Prize winner will most likely invite you to take a different path.

Now, if we think just a little deeper here we can see that the actual aim of having a goal is to give us a way to organize our actions. In an honest sense, the goal of setting the goal is an action itself. Of course we want the goal to happen, but the focus it generates is the necessary action itself. The reason setting a goal is important is that it births our actions, and **Action's the Thing!**

What is Action?

We may not be asking the perfect question here, but we are definitely considering an important insight. You are on the way to developing *The One Success Habit*, and by now you should be getting the idea that it is about action itself.
What is action? Well, action is doing something. It is motion or movement. Action can be a new thought, a step, a phone call, a drawing, a typed sentence, a wink, a brush stroke, or just writing a check. None of this actually helps us that much without considering a little philosophy.

Philosophy simply means 'the love of wisdom', so if you are on the path of becoming wise, then you must become a 'philosopher' of some sort. However, please remember that both philosophers and restaurants come in all shapes and sizes.

Some of the high-end philosophers have seen that there is a relationship with action that is worth noting. Action is connected to two key elements:

Time & Change

Time in some ways is simply a measure of change. Even the movement of a second hand on a clock is a change; as is the place of the sun overhead, or the wind in a sail. Change means nothing more than something is different than before. Something was one way or in one spot, but is now another way or in another spot.

The conversation about action and time and change is important because it allows us to think about what we are doing to succeed in profound and effective ways. Pause for a moment and consider something you want to accomplish. What is your next action? How can your next action be improved by thinking about time and change? The answer is found in Kaizen.

Kaizen Helps Find the Right Action

The quality movement birthed in the 1970s and spear-headed by Toyota made use of the term Kaizen; which roughly combined the ideas of change and virtue. Kaizen, therefore is about changing things for the better; essentially the quest for perfection.

Lao Tzu is credited with observing that "The journey of a thousand miles begins with a single step."

Kaizen itself is about 'continuous' improvement on the way toward a practical kind of perfection. Continuous improvement comes about through small changes, or rather, small changes in time. In developing *The One Success Habit*, Kaizen comes in very handy. We often don't take actions because the actions are simply too big; that is, the action we think we need to take is too much change in too short a time.

Remember, **Action's the Thing**! Also, action is about change and time. It therefore becomes pretty simple to see that a major reason we don't take action is that our next action will simply take too much time or is too big of a change to do next.

The cure is simple.

Start with Easy: *The Next Step is Never Hard*

I have notoriously sensitive feet; even walking on sand hurts! So, I would have to change Lao Tzu's insight to,

"The journey of a thousand miles starts with putting on my sandals."

In any project or process, the next step is always the easiest of all the remaining steps. Climbing a mountain by jumping to a ledge halfway up the cliff is insurmountable and overwhelming. Stepping up onto the next shelf just in front of you is the right move to climb the mountain.

In truth, *The Next Step is Never Hard*. If you find the next step to be hard, then it isn't the real next step.

Writing the paper may be hard, but turning on the computer is not. Writing 25 pages may be hard, but writing the next sentence is not. True?

We Reap as We Sow

The Bible said it this way a couple of thousand years ago,

> *Don't be misled: No one makes a fool of God. What a person plants, he will harvest. The person who plants selfishness, ignoring the needs of others—ignoring God!— harvests a crop of weeds. All he'll have to show for his life is weeds! But the one who plants in response to God, letting God's Spirit do the growth work in him, harvests a crop of real life, eternal life. (Galatians 6:7–8,* The Message)

The principle borrows from agriculture and notes that a seed planted produces a crop. If you want wheat, you plant grains of wheat. If you want more wheat, plant more grains. Practically speaking what does this mean to you personally? What is it that you want to see happen? If you want to be a musician, you still will need to learn the scale like Mozart did. If you want to promote a cause, you will need to learn a little something about sales or communication. Can you start with a book? If that is too big, can you start with a better question? Is there someone to take to lunch? *The next step is never hard. The journey of a thousand miles begins with putting on your sandals.*

Action is the thing. Action is about time and change. Action can be very small, but a single action can lead to a great harvest in the area you want to succeed. Here's a place to begin:

What action could you take next toward your success? What smaller action would lead to that action? What even easier action would lead to that action?

Action's the Thing, but action won't happen consistently unless you can say, "Yes," to the following question...

Chapter 3

Do You Really Understand Motivation?

A man went fishing one day. He looked over the side of his boat and saw a snake with a frog in its mouth. Feeling sorry for the frog, he reached down, gently took the frog from the snake, and set the frog free. But then he felt sorry for the snake. He looked around the boat, but he had no food. All he had was a bottle of bourbon. So he opened the bottle and gave the snake a few shots. The snake went off happy, the frog was happy, and the man was happy to have performed such good deeds. He thought everything was great until about ten minutes passed and he heard something knock against the side of the boat. With stunned disbelief, the fisherman looked down and saw the snake was back with two frogs! (Fred R. Lybrand, *The Absolute Quickest Way to Help Your Child Change*, p. 54).

The frog, the snake, and the man had different motives. Why do you do what you do? What motivates you? *The One Success Habit* has everything to do with motivation. Once we realize that **Action's the Thing**, we can appreciate the value of motivation. Motivation, at its root, is all about motion. It is not only what gets us in motion, but it is what keeps us moving in the right direction.

It's a funny thing, but most of the criticism toward 'motivational speakers' is that they are just about getting people pumped up.

Of course, as we saw in Chapter 1, the goal of most self-help speakers is to get people to act. If you act, something will happen. If you fail to act, nothing will happen. It stands to reason, therefore, that speakers would actually try to motivate the audience. Motivation means motion. Indeed, wouldn't any speaker be a disappointment who didn't motivate the audience?

The real complaint is that the motivational pep talk doesn't last. It is just called a 'rah–rah' event; meaning, as a derogatory statement, that it costs money, but has no effect. The funny thing about motivation, however, is that all motivation goes away in the course of time. We are hungry…we are motivated…we take action and eat…we aren't hungry…we aren't motivated. It happens with everything from the most basic needs to the wildest desires.

The challenge we face in developing the habit we need for success is that we must learn to oversee our own motivation. People who know how to keep themselves motivated tend to succeed. People who know how to keep others motivated tend to lead. There is a simple mistake most of us make about motivation, which we'll refer to as…

The Misunderstanding of Motivation

One of my mentors, Robert Fritz, helped me see the misunderstanding regarding motivation. Motivation is never just one thing.

Motivation is always about a relationship between two or more things. Really, except for God, there is no single-point causality.

The easiest way to show that motivation involves more than one thing is to point to the example of advertising. We all have seen commercials involving beautiful women and cool cars. A visitor to earth who is unfamiliar with our ways would conclude that we are probably selling the women in the commercials, but they would be wrong. The advertisements are selling the cars by implying that owning the car leads to getting women. The fact of the matter is that I am happily married and don't need a car. Do you think these commercials have any effect on me? You'd be wrong if you said, "Yes." Unless I need a car (or a woman, I guess) it doesn't motivate me. For motivation to happen there must be a relationship between what is being offered and what is desired. Face it; lactose intolerant people aren't motivated by the 'Got Milk' commercials. Singles without kids aren't motivated by 'Huggies' commercials. And, vegans aren't motivated by "Jimmie Dean Sausage' commercials.

When it comes to goals, the same thing applies. As we know, a goal is a desired outcome. Yet, unless one is aware of the absence of the outcome in the real world, then he isn't motivated.

Motivation is generated by the difference (or discrepancy) between what you want and what you have.

If you want there to be money in your bank account, but you also think there is money...then, you have no motivation to go online and check. However, if someone calls and says your check bounced due to a lack of funds...a BIG motivation to go online and check your account right now appears.

Motivation is always a relationship between what you want and what you have; if you have what you want you aren't motivated. But, if you don't have what you want, then you are motivated. The only tweak here is to mention that if you think what you want is a complete impossibility, then you won't be motivated. In this case there is no relationship between what you want and what you have.

So, to be motivated you must (1) Desire something you think is not impossible to have or create, and (2) Know that you do not currently have it. It is easy to just think of these two things as (1) **There**, and (2) **Here**. **There** is what you want or where you want to go in the future. **Here** is where you are or where you are starting in the present.

The mistake is to think that just looking at what you want (money, success, stuff, contribution, relationship, etc.) is real motivation. The truth is that looking at BOTH what you want and what you currently have (or lack) is what truly motivates. If you are a leader, the same issue applies. Helping those you lead see BOTH the vision AND how things are in the present, helps get everyone motivated in the same direction together. On the most basic level, all motivation is about having a better future. Even when people are motivated not to change it is because they think 'here' is the 'there' they want in the future.

Covey's Mistake

As I write these words I am hesitant and humbled to even question someone of Steven Covey's stature. With his passing we lost a legend in the business and human productivity worlds. What a helpful contribution he made with the 7 Habits information and his principle-centered training. What a nice correction to invite us back to a human values based way to approach the topic of success in our daily lives.

Covey's contribution notwithstanding, I think he made a bit of mistake in the midst of the habits. Since his lingo is now cultural common knowledge, it might take a little work to think clearly on this one. Covey offers the idea of pursing what he calls 'Quadrant II' items in our planning and labors. The Quadrant II mistake cuts to the heart of the issue in *The One Success Habit*.

Steven Covey offers a matrix with four components--- Urgent, Non-Urgent, Important, and Non-Important. The idea in his grid is that the urgent things in our lives tyrannize us and often cause us to neglect the important things. He recommends that we focus on the Non-Urgent-but-Important matters in our lives. These are the things in Quadrant II, and he offers that getting ourselves to focus here makes the difference.

Frankly, Covey's mistake really does feel right at first glance. Surely we all feel the sense that we are caught up focusing on things that are pressing but don't really matter.

Imagine if we could get ourselves to focus on things we know are important, but that also do not present themselves as urgent just now. How would your life change if you worked on the really 'important' things now?

But hold on. A second take reveals a mistake in the way Covey thinks about the point (apologies again). Is there such a thing as something that is Urgent-but-Not-Important? Really? No, really? Name it. Better yet, if you can think of something you are doing that is Urgent-but-Not-Important, then I want to pose a simple question,

WHY DO IT IF IT IS UNIMPORTANT?

A leader in a sizeable Energy company who is a friend of mine wrestled a little here with me not too long ago. He said that one of the earlier companies he 'learned the ropes in' always seemed to have everyone busy with urgent things that weren't all that important. In fact, he said this was the biggest complaint from all the employees. I responded by asking him, "So why do them? Why not drop them?"

As he thought about it I asked him a further question, "What would have happened if all those 'unimportant' things had just been dropped?" He responded with a thoughtful, "I see the point."

The point is that the 'unimportant' stuff in that company was the reporting that kept all the information they needed for every decision in a current-and-ready format. If the information about all the drilling, production, royalties, overrides, etc., wasn't current and available---the whole company would fall into disarray in a few short weeks!

The truth is that if it is urgent it is important (and vise-versa)!

At this writing, I have a couple of sons still at home who are in their mid and late teens. Both of them admit that it is important for them to find the right life partner in a wife. They are very pro-women and pro-marriage. However, since they don't want to consider marriage until they are a bit older, it isn't urgent! In fact, both of them largely don't see the point of exclusively dating someone until they are closer to a marriageable time in their lives. Marriage is important to them…but not NOW. Because marriage isn't urgent it actually is not IMPORTANT to them right now.

Do you see the heart of Covey's mistake? If something isn't important now (urgent), it really isn't important at all. Of course, it WILL BE important when it is important; and quite frankly, it will be URGENT when it is REALLY IMPORTANT.

Urgent and important go hand-in-hand in relationship to time; it is the deadline that makes the difference. **To say something *will be* important someday is to say it is not important *now*.** That truly is the distinction.

If something doesn't need to be done now it just simply isn't important…go ahead…admit it! On the other hand, if it is honestly urgent then why not admit it is also important to you right now? Again, if you think what you are working on is URGENT-BUT-NOT-IMPORTANT, then ask yourself,

WHY DO IT IF IT IS UNIMPORTANT?

In fact, you could at least ask yourself, "Why do it NOW if it is unimportant?" I'm sure this is what Covey was trying to get us to see. But, it can't be urgent if it is unimportant. The reason it is urgent is that it is important to you at the moment. *The One Success Habit* will focus on appreciating the fact that unless what you are working on isn't urgent it really isn't important either. This brings us to a simple question...

Why Does It Matter to Know Motivation Isn't Just One Thing?

Gaining the insight that motivation is about a relationship between what you want and what you currently have will dramatically allow you to focus on the success you want. In fact, there are really three elements in motivation:

1. What you want (the goal)
2. What you have (the current situation)
3. Time (a chosen deadline)

Motivation always involves all three of these elements. If you don't want anything, then you won't be motivated (but you might be happy). If you want something, but don't know you don't have it, you won't be motivated either (and you might be happy-though-deceived). If you want something and know you don't have it, but also think you have FOREVER to get it; you won't be particularly motivated as well.

The key is to have a clear idea of (1) What you want; (2) The fact that you don't have it; and (3) When you will have (or create) it by. These three things, in a solid relationship with one another, will generate motivation. Said simply, it is a matter of the relationship between HERE, THERE, and DEADLINE.

We can see this as the Delta of Motivation:

DEADLINE

Take a moment now and think about something you are motivated to accomplish. Aren't all three in place?

The 4ᵗʰ Element

Actually, there is another element that we can add to the Delta of Motivation. The fourth item is a plan. The plan connects the other three elements together. We like to refer it as the "path" that will take you from Here to There. Having a fair idea of how to begin is often the final missing ingredient for many people.

Haven't you known what you wanted to do but had no idea how to begin? That's the issue sometimes.

The plan needn't be perfect; it just needs to be something that is likely to get you to the result you desire. It is very much like walking a path, along which you adjust the whole way around rocks and limbs and other obstacles.

All plans are adjusted along the way, so don't over commit. Nonetheless, adding a basic strategy to the other three elements can often be the tipping point for action. And, of course, ACTION'S THE THING! Planning usually means you, paper, pen, and brain answering one question, "What do I need to do to make this happen?"

Here's a complete view of the Delta of Motivation:

Take another moment and consider something you want to be more motivated to accomplish. Are all four elements clear? Really? Work it out on a piece of scrap paper and you'll see what's missing.

Next, if you are going to develop *The One Success Habit*, then you really need to answer this…

Chapter 4

What Really is a Habit?

Over the years I've come to appreciate how difficult it is to think crooked and walk straight. Almost everything we do or do not do is standing on a set of facts, beliefs, assumptions, and perceptions. Generally speaking we call this "thinking." How we think affects our actions, these actions in turn produce our results. If you are going to succeed in developing *The One Success Habit*, then you really need to know how to think about habits.

The summer before my 6th grade year when I was twelve years old, I picked up a bad habit; I started smoking cigarettes. Cigarette smoking is apparently one of the most difficult habits to shake, and no doubt in one summer, at the edge of puberty, I hadn't deeply engrained a smoking habit. Yet, in one moment, a new way to think changed everything for me.

Now, understand that my parents smoked along with almost all of their friends. Back then smoking was common and no one could see why charring your lungs as black as mold was a bad idea.

Thomas and I used to sneak off in one of our boats (we were pals with family lake cabins near each other) and make our way up the undeveloped part of Choccolocca Creek in Alabama. Just at a right spot we would tie up our boat and climb an overgrown red-clay path up to a country store on Highway 77. That's where we bought our cigarettes; no carding, no questions, no problem. So we sneaked off and acted as cool as our imaginations would allow. We smoked at home. We smoked in the woods near our house. We smoked plenty. We liked it, we were *men*, and we were getting away with it!

In the early part of the fall after school started, my older brother Stephen (he was four years older and in the 10th grade) came in while I was doing my homework one evening. He told me he heard that I was smoking. I can't remember if he got on to me too, but I clearly remember that he told me how disappointed he was about it. In one stellar moment my brother had given me a complete change in my thinking. I have never smoked a cigarette since that day we talked.

How we think about things can dramatically affect what we do, and how we think about habits can dramatically affect what we do with them.

Defining a Habit

I'm sure there are plenty of textbook definitions; however, I want this chapter to be more useful and practical than it is academic. Here's how I want to invite you to think about habits as a practical-thinker:

A habit is a pattern of behavior that is consistently and automatically followed; using no conscious thought or conscious willpower.

Okay, maybe that is a little academic, but it can be really useful. If you are going to develop *The One Success Habit*, then don't you think it will be helpful to know when you actually have the habit?

The key in the definition is the word pattern, which means a sequence that is followed over-and-over again. It is reliable, which means the result is reliable too. If you are one of those folks who say the words "please" and "thank you," then I'm pretty sure you have that down as a habit. The reason you have it is that you learned that including those words got you something you wanted in the most efficient way possible. Indeed, all of your use of language, as well as your dialect, is nothing more (or less) than a language habit.

When you talk over dinner about a variety of subjects you are engaged in picking and choosing words according to patterns you've learned (called grammar). You are not consciously using your willpower or your thoughts to put these words together in meaningful ways. If you are confusing when you talk it is largely because you don't have good habits for communicating. In fact, you probably have poor habits in your thinking which just show up clearly in what you say!

Enough about definitions don't you think? Let's move on to look at a few things we need to understand about every habit.

A Habit is a Given

There is no easy way to tell you this if you fancy yourself as a free-spirit, unchained and unrestrained by anyone or anything; you still have habits. In fact, if you get up and aim to be spontaneous every day---you will develop a habit for daily spontaneity! It is a given, that as a part of the reality of how things go that we all have habits. It is a given we will sleep, eat, hurt, and have habits. Regardless of your own convictions about how you got to earth, there is universal agreement that there is some impressive intelligence behind our design. Habits allow us to learn-for-good a variety of skills and processes that make us free to think, produce, enjoy, and create. Without the ability to create a habit we'd daily have to repeat learning the things we need just for survival. In the place of habits we would need many more pre-installed instincts, which would also mean we would repeat our daily survival and functional activities. In some profound ways, the ability to learn habits is what contributes to all human progress.

Admitting habits are a given allows us to do a couple of important   things

1. We can quit fighting the fact that we are creatures with habits.
2. We can make use of this knowledge to aid our success.

The second point is particularly useful to hold near our hearts.

For example, gravity is also a given. Once we own up to it, we can start working with it. From wake-boarding to world travel to weather satellites, understanding the nature of gravity mathematically and practically allows us to get some impressive results. Accepting the reality of habits allows us to make use of them as well.

A Habit is Morally Neutral

When we think about a habit as morally neutral, we mean that it isn't good or bad in itself. We can have a good habit or a bad habit, but our bent toward having habits isn't to be blamed or glorified. Habits can be helpful or hurtful, to others as well as to you. Ignoring the bent to develop habits might be a bit of a moral flaw since you will give over the power to direct your habits to the whim of the circumstance. Maybe that helps, but more than likely it hurts. If you actually can choose your habits, then you can become responsible rather than remain a victim.

A Habit is Always Created

Researchers will never find a gene for your best and worst habits. If they do you can finally know that there is a conspiracy against you! A genetic bent isn't a habit anyway. There may be a habit gene, but all your habits are created. As I mentioned before, you are hardwired for language, but you can grow up and learn the habit of the language around you.

Each habit has to be formed in a context, and comes about through one of two mechanisms:

1. A habit can be created unintentionally
2. A habit can be created intentionally

Unintentional habits are automatic behavior patterns which develop WITHOUT our awareness. Often they develop because we are innocent (especially as children) and don't realize we are repeating a pattern of action until it is deeply wired into our brains. Sometimes they develop because we aren't thinking any farther than the next moment. The rock band KISS offers a path to a rock-and-roll habit when it sings, "*I want to rock-and-roll all night...and party every day.*" If you move from rock-and-roll at night to a party every day...you'll pretty soon have quite a habit! If you develop the rock-and-roll habit it will be because you are trying to live out the words to a song you are singing without paying attention to what you are doing. Of course, this is just an illustration, right?

Intentional habits are automatic behavior patterns which develop WITH our awareness. We are not innocent, we are responsible. We are engaged in repeating an action (or set of actions) until it (they) becomes automatic. If we stick with our musical theme, you could sing along with Julie Andrews in *The Sound of Music*, "...when the dog bites, when the bee stings, when I'm feeling sad..." and continue on to think about a 'few of your favorite things'---then you won't feel so bad! A habit of singing a song to get your mind on better things is an example of an intentional habit because you are aware of what you are doing until it becomes automatic.

Yes, habits are created. How they are created is multi-staged. However, the one thing you can keep in mind is that habits normally form through small steps. Just as we learned about both **Action's the Thing** and Kaizen (Chapter 2), we understand small steps lead to big results. Habits form one cigarette, one voice lesson, and one salute at a time.

A Habit is a Servant

A habit is meant to serve you personally. If it had a motive, then your wish would be its command. The design within us to form habits is clearly there for our good.
The power of a habit is to give you freedom to think and act in complicated ways. How could we ever fall in love or talk things through while driving a car if we had to consciously focus on driving every moment?

A habit is always directed toward one thing: good feelings. If you wish, take time to reflect on the profound nature of everyone's orientation to pursue what will feel good. Even in the areas of responsibility and values good feelings are at the heart of it all. Hey, who wants to feel bad anyway? Oh yes, masochists do…except, it feels good to them to feel so awful. Blues music is about feeling good about feeling bad. Good parents are trying to help children mature so the children will feel good someday about life…and so…the parents will also feel good about having had the kids.

It is an inescapable reality that seems self-centered. Self-interest, however, is a little different than being self-centered. Logical people are usually the last to admit this fact. Yet, the most logical-and-anti-feelings person has to admit in their most honest moments that it 'feels good' to think clearly!

It is also true that the most destructive habits, like the addictions to alcohol or drugs, have as their aim good feelings. On the physical side of becoming addicted the body feels miserable without the substance of choice. Taking a drink or a hit 'feels good' by contrast, though all an addict is hoping for is to feel okay for a little while. The initial euphoria of the drug usually leaves after the habit is established.

The truth that a habit aims at a 'good feeling' turns out to be a helpful insight when we are intentional about our habits. Clarifying the 'good feelings' the habit will give us can keep us on track until the habit is automatic.

A Habit Can Become a Master

Nothing much needs to be said here, but it is worth noting that although a habit is supposed to serve us, we can turn around and become our habit's servant.
When we are mastered by a habit we normally call it an addiction. While most addictions are harmful, some such as running can be helpful (for the most part). The challenge with becoming a servant to a habit is that we yield our freedom as human beings. The ancient wisdom from the Bible says it this way,

Just because something is technically legal doesn't mean that it's spiritually appropriate. If I went around doing whatever I thought I could get by with, I'd be a slave to my whims. (1 Corinthians 6:12, The Message)

Being enslaved to a habit isn't helpful, nor does it feel good over time. If we see habits as servants then we can dismiss them if they aren't producing good things for our lives. If we see habits as masters, then there isn't a very easy way to 'get fired' or become free.

A Habit is Easier to Replace than Destroy

There is an odd paradox our brains play out, but only because of our misunderstanding. Have you ever noticed how trying not to think about something makes you think about it? A thought, an issue, or a song can get 'stuck in our heads' and nothing seems to be able to make it go away. Our kids often have come in and complained that they have a song on their mind that just won't go away. I tell them I can cure it if they'd like me to. Once they agree, I start singing, "When you're with the Flintstones you'll have a yabba-dabba-do time..." Of course, after a few noisy choruses they no longer are singing the former song, they are on the Flintstones song! When it comes to our mind it is all about focus. Trying 'not to think' about something is to still think about it. To think about something else is to think about something else entirely. Your brain just wants something to do---so tell it what you want.

Now you know all you really need to know about unwanted habits. Trying to kill a habit usually just reinforces it. Instead, it is far more effective to establish a habit on top of the one you want to remove from your life.

A habit in a particular area is probably a given, so why not choose what the habit will be? As I grew up in Alabama I ran into a few people who didn't exactly use the kind of grammar I wanted to use (it's the same in Texas too!). For a while I formed the habit of correcting people in the moment they misspoke, but I found that to be a pretty unsafe way to keep my own grammar straight and my friendships intact. So, I came up with a replacement habit that I continue to this day. If I hear someone say something in a way I don't want to speak (e.g. "me and Jimmy is going to the creek"), I simply say it correctly to myself. I follow this habit in daily conversations, while watching television, listening to the radio, or while at a tractor pull. Well, you get my point.

How to Create a Habit

Let's conclude this chapter with a few thoughts on how to create a habit, intentionally of course. Here are the basic steps:

1. Make your goal of a new habit match the definition. It is a habit when it is automatic, requiring no conscious thought or will power.
2. Clarify why the new habit is in your best interest. What will your future life be like and how will you feel when it is automatic?

3. Consider and accept exactly which good feelings the habit will add to your life.
4. Design a pattern of actions that involves easy steps from the very start.
5. Repeat the pattern every time the situation occurs
6. If you fail…go back and repeat the pattern on top of the failed attempt (in football they call this "running the play until you get it right").
7. Tweak the pattern if you find a better way.
8. Keep repeating the pattern until it is automatic.

Often we hear that it takes twenty-one days to establish a habit. I haven't been able to verify this magic number, but I like it as a goal. The real trick is to simply aim to never ever (no never) have an exception to your pattern. If you allow exceptions then it is not a habit. This may begin on the first attempt. I've noticed that most small children will have a new habit if they can do something five days in a row. Other habits can take up to four or five months to establish. Chances are it varies with the person and the specific habit. The key is to think in terms of getting it to be automatic, not in terms of a number of attempts.

When we get to *The One Success Habit*, we'll see how to put everything together in a personalized plan.

For now, just play around with your habits & know the next part of the answer follows asking…

Chapter 5

What is the Solution?

Circumstances are the rulers of the weak; they are but the instruments of the wise. -Samuel Lover

The system is the solution. -Michael Gerber

Honestly, there is no information in this book that will impact your day-to-day life more than what you are about to learn here. This chapter isn't easy, but it is worth its weight in gold. You are about to see how the world works and what you can do to function better in it. More than anything, thinking about systems is really just a way to think about how things happen. Once you know what causes things to happen, then you'll know what you can do to get in on the action! We need to take a little detour first and consider a profound question:

What if we really are responsible for everything that happens to us?

Now, before you either push back or get too excited with agreement, just think about it. I've asked plenty of people this question to find out how it makes them feel. Most people say considering this to be true makes them feel scared or uncomfortable.

Their answer is really interesting because it makes me feel things like 'freedom, empowerment, and not being a victim in life. I'm sure the question makes you feel responsible, which could be scary or empowering, depending on your point of view.

Of course God is in charge and things happen, but that's not what this question is asking about or looking at. You do basically play the hand you are dealt, but what if that makes a huge difference? Saying, "Hit me," can lead to winning or losing. Is winning the hand the dealer's fault or your own?

Here's the test to figure out if this thought about personal responsibility is true or not---simply notice that a different action you could take would change what happens. If your action would change what happens, then we can safely conclude that you really are responsible for everything that happens to you. I know you can't control if it rains on you, but you can control whether or not you keep getting wet.

The question does not say that you can be anything or have everything you want (well...it could say that, but it doesn't have to). But, it does AT LEAST say that what finally happens to you, given the context that appears around you, is the result of your own actions or reactions.

Then again, what happens around you could also be affected by your actions. What if you walk away from the blackjack table or move to where it never rains?

Systems thinking is really about this last part; walking away from the table or moving to a different card game.

You can understand and change the systems that make up the context that appears around you. We aren't talking about a set of ethereal metaphysical secrets that force the Universe to help us; we are talking about real day-to-day life on the planet. What if we really are responsible for everything that happens to us?

Ready? Let's get started with the next best question,

What is a System?

A system is simply a more accurate way to explain what happens in this universe. We can talk about cause-and-effect in different ways, but nothing explains it like a system does. For example, why does it rain? Well, moist air is hit by colder air, which then condenses to cause rain. That is right, but it really isn't the whole story. There are a number of weather systems normally in play, never mind that a hurricane is a different beast altogether.

We normally think that

A…causes…B…causes…C.

I kick the dog…the dog chases the cat…the cat scratches the window screen in its escape. But, it really is not that simplistic. There are many things in play between cats, dogs, and screens.

Systems thinking looks at what happens this way:

A…affects…B…affects…C…affects D…which is affecting B…which is affecting A back…while A is really affecting C…which is affecting Z, X, and Q.

Well, you get the idea. There are many parts in play. If you think about your success in life the same game is in play for you. Just the simple matter of making a sale can involve dozens of elements besides the customer, the product, and you; the weather, the upcoming vacation, the economy, the call from the school about your customer's son…EACH IMPACTS ALL, and the sale itself.

Frankly, if you want to succeed you need to understand how thinking in terms of systems can change everything for you.

Franchises are an obvious example for us to see the power of systems in the hands of regular people. In a franchise like Chick-fil-A, almost all of the systems are automated and the processes are established. Chick-fil-A has ways to promote the store, clean things, pour drinks, cook waffle fries, and greet customers.

All of these things have been standardized and tweaked so that every franchise is a more-or-less guaranteed success machine. Of course they may vary a little from store to store, but that is influenced by the local economy, the age of the store in an area, the style of the operator, and the location.

If you own a Chick-fil-A, and do it like they say, you will very likely do great. The reason you will do great is that you are following a system, and the system will do what it is made to do. If you try to violate the franchise system because you think you know better than they do…you are definitely in the wrong business. **The system is the solution.**

There is No Such Thing as a Bad System

Systems are not personal, so they are not immoral and they are not broken; there is no such thing as a bad system. We say things like, "The system is broken," but we really don't mean what it sounds like.

Here's an example from the 1970s. Way back before quality took root, American car companies didn't always put out a good product. One particular automobile that was supremely marginal was the Chevette. It was supposed to be Detroit's answer to giving us an American made economical car, but it was largely a piece of junk. I'm not trying to offend anyone here, but clearly it had no future. A friend of mine shared with me that when he was a car sales person in the Dallas area, they had to run Chevettes for about 30 minutes before they opened for business during the winter months--- just so the car would start for a potential customer!

So, wasn't the 'Chevette-Factory-System' broken to put out such a thing? Wasn't it a bad system? Not at all! It was a very good system for putting out a very consistent piece of junk.

If you wanted to put out a poor car you would want to mimic the Chevette-building system; poor design, poor materials, untrained workers for that assembly, etc. Actually, I don't know the system (they were probably great workers), but I do know Chevrolet had a process that put out the same product again and again. If I wanted to put out a bad product, then the easy way to do so would be to copy-and-follow another system that gets the 'bad' result I want.

Think about this with your family growing up, or your church, or your approach to leadership. What system are you copying? Did it produce the results you wanted? Will it in the future? Are you beginning to see why we are bothering with talking about systems in learning *The One Success Habit (You Can't Do Without)*? Here's what you really need to know…

The System is the Solution

If you want a different result just create a different system. Einstein's remark that, "Insanity is doing the same thing over and over, but expecting a different result," is just right. As one of my professors would have said, "He hit the nail with his head." The results you keep getting in life come from the systems you have around you and the systems you are using. If your system is to try a different sales approach every single day, then your results will vary wildly. If your system for parenting isn't producing the results you want, it isn't your child's fault. Frankly, if your house doesn't stay clean it isn't the house's fault either.

A system is a combination of influences that produce a consistent result. If you put a new system in place, you will decidedly get a new result. That's really all there is to it, except...

How Do You Create a System?

Sam Carpenter has written a very practical book on this topic entitled *Work the System*. In it he explains how he learned and applies systems thinking to his life and business. His keen observation is that even though a system already has all the parts interacting with one another, you build a system by a sequence of steps; you might as well call this a procedure. A procedure is a game plan for how to proceed. A procedure helps a system develop and settle in to operating in a predictable way. Kaizen tells us that we can make small tweaks to the procedures we set up to move toward constant improvement.

Here's an example of using a systems approach to solve a problem we were facing with our three sons and their mother. Mom complained that the boys (ages 13, 16, and 18 at the time) weren't doing what she asked them to do. The boys said that Mom wasn't punishing them enough (yes one of them actually said this) or that they were "just about to do" what she asked, but just hadn't gotten to it yet.

After quizzing everyone a bit we figured out that there was no clear deadline given. At first it seemed that Mom just needed to give a deadline. But that isn't real systems thinking---that's just laying another burden on Mom.

So, here is a copy of the procedure we wrote down and put on the refrigerator. It has the three parts Sam Carpenter recommends; the objective, the guidelines, and the steps.

Parenting Strategy: *Getting Task Requests Done*
Lybrand Boys
September 1st

Objective:

To have the boys do tasks their mother asks of them in a timely and proper fashion, and without her constantly reminding them

Guidelines/Principles:

✓ Children obey your parents … for this is right
✓ Definition of a man… "One who rejects passivity…"
✓ Whatever you do in word or deed… do unto the Lord
✓ Keep your word
✓ Honor your mother…

Procedure:

1. 5:00pm is the deadline for any task Mother asks you to do; unless Mother sets a specific

deadline

2. If she asks you to do something past 5:00pm without setting a deadline, then it will be due the next day at 5:00pm

3. We'll consider (in the future) if 'not being allowed to leave until the task is done' will need to be added to the procedure

*** We'll review constantly, but especially at a meeting on October 1st (in a month)

*** My wife Jody and I have a few hobbies; including family-courses applying these principles (and a few others) is free at www.homeandschoolsuccess.com

_____

The truth of the matter is that it instantly changed everything. Our boys weren't lazy or rebellious; they were just in need of some kind of consistent and clear instructions.

Mom was in a system that gave a clear direction but no clear deadline (remember TIME is one of the keys to motivation).

The Point

I am sorry for working through this part for some of you. But, even though it may not fascinate you, it will change your life.

If you are going to develop *The One Success Habit*, then you must have a basic understanding of why what I am going to encourage you to do will develop the habit. My greatest hope is for you to feel good about the success you have begun to see every day once you have *The One Success Habit* in your life; but, if you don't build a system for your success, I don't see how you will ever really succeed.

What if we really are responsible for everything that happens to us?

If we will build the right systems around us the magic just might happen. But, we all need to embrace and use one of the great secrets of One Habit warfare...

Chapter 6

Do You Know Your #1 Enemy?

To thine own self be true, and it must follow, as the night the day, thou canst not then be false to any man.
-William Shakespeare

Socrates simply said, "Know thyself." In either case, they were both on to something. Knowing oneself makes sense in the quest to succeed because it positions you to make use of your talents while minimizing your weaknesses. The other side is to know your enemy.

The history of warfare underscores the priority of genuinely understanding the enemy. Myths, legends, and movies repeat this truism nonstop. The fall of Troy to the Greeks is said to have occurred because 'the horse' played into the god-worship of the day. Football teams spend countless hours watching film and thinking through the assets and liabilities of each week's opponent.

If **Action's the Thing**, then wouldn't it stand to reason that understanding the enemy is a smart move? Doctors do this all the time by making a proper diagnosis. If you can clearly know the nature of the disease, the course of treatment is all-but-dictated.

How to Defeat an Enemy

In medicine it stands out as perhaps the biggest faux pas in recent history. In fact, you may still be operating under the falsehood that stomach ulcers are caused by stress. It still occurs in television shows---an overweight and 'stressed out' individual is told to back off on spicy foods and to reduce overall stress in his life. The notion is that stress is causing the stomach ulcer. In 1982 medical doctors figured out what veterinarians had known for years about ulcers in hogs. Stomach ulcers are caused by the bacterium Helicobacter which can thrive in the stomach (who would've thought?).

When we thought the enemy was stress, the treatment was for stress. When we discovered the enemy was a kind of bacteria, the treatment became an antibiotic.

The way you defeat an enemy is to exploit the enemy. The exploitation, however, can only be effective if you FIRST UNDERSTAND the enemy. One obvious approach to defeating an enemy can be charted with a few simple steps:

1. Understand your enemy
2. Tactically consider his weaknesses
3. Tactically consider your resources
4. Strategically attack his weaknesses with your resources

The #1 Enemy of Action

When we ask people what the enemy of action is, they tell us things like 'inaction', 'no motivation', and 'not knowing what to do next'. All of these belong in the conversation, but they really don't strike at the heart of the issue. Inaction, for example, is simply the opposite of action. Thinking inaction is the problem is like saying marriage is the enemy of being single.

Motivation itself is certainly an issue, which is why we dedicated an entire chapter to the topic. But, if motivation leads to action, then action just flows from the motivation. Lack of motivation could be more precise, but it is really like saying the enemy of action is inaction.

Not knowing what to do is also a prime candidate as the enemy of action, but plenty of people go out and take lots of actions without much of a plan at all.

I believe the enemy of action is both surprising and obvious.

The #1 Enemy of Action is Dishonesty

Please bear in mind that we are thinking about why we as individuals do not take action on things we honestly think we should take action on. We aren't looking at the notion of being 'inactive' as a character flaw. Instead, we are looking at why you tell yourself you are going to get going on that important project, but manage to find many ways to avoid starting.

When you don't take action although you think you will, you are under the influence of a vast conspiracy. Your personal failure to be honest teams up with your personal failure to take action. If you are like most people when they are introduced to this idea concerning dishonesty, you are probably skeptical. Of course, that is the nature of your lack of honesty on the matter!

Before you reject dishonesty as the enemy of action, please listen when I tell you it is not your fault. You come by this sort of lying very honestly (so to speak). You really have been innocent up to this point, which is to say that you have not been aware of what is happening.

First, let me prove to you that dishonesty is the enemy. You can actually prove it to yourself if you will simply go through a normal day in your mind. The story goes like this--- you decide what you want to do that day, put it on a list, put it in order, get to work, and find out by the end of the day it (or many 'its') just didn't happen. Of course there were reasons; in fact there were thousands of reasons. You were interrupted by a crisis, the boss threw a fresh project at you, the kids came in with a problem, your spouse reminded you of a promise you made last week, a golf game came up and you haven't played in weeks…and the list goes on.

Think about it slowly and carefully. Did you really think you would be able to get everything on your list done?

Oh…you didn't get your list done because you don't use it for what you'll get done, but as a reminder of what needs doing. So it isn't a 'Going To-Do' list, it is a 'Need To-Do' list.

Another option is that you said you were going to get it done, but for similar reasons it just didn't happen. You promised yourself, but you didn't keep the promise. Can you see that all of this is about not being entirely honest with yourself (remember Shakespeare's point)? **What would it be like if you knew exactly what you would get done and could guarantee you would do what you said?** Shortly we will look at how we can learn to be honest, but for now we just need to own up to the fact that we fib to ourselves (and probably others too?) all the time. We not only say we are going to do something, but we actually believe ourselves! In brutal moments when we feel safe because no one is looking, we can all admit that there are just certain things in a particular day we honestly are not going to do. If we don't recognize dishonesty is the enemy, how will we ever recognize the cure?

Why Are We Dishonest With Ourselves?

A first glance suggests that we are simply a bunch of optimists; our eyes are bigger than our stomachs, our hopes are bigger than our capacity. You know, 'be optimistic'---attack Moby Dick with the tartar sauce in your backpack! Yet, is it simply that we are just a bunch of fibbers because we are trying to teach ourselves to be optimists?

A second explanation is that we all feel a terrific amount of pressure from everyone who is counting on us including our boss, spouse, kids, friends, and the government. With all that pressure we just say what we need to say so they won't be mad at us (or at least will leave us alone). We also really mean to get it done, that's our intention (did I mention optimism?). I'm sure the need for approval mixes in here somewhere, but truthfully, when you think it through, haven't you noticed that these people you don't want mad at you will get mad when you don't do what you promised?

The best explanation is that we simply aren't in the habit of telling ourselves the truth. An honesty habit will change everything. However, underneath this habit is a simple and honest misunderstanding about your will. The will is called by many names such as our 'chooser', our 'volition', or our 'decider'. We even have ways to speak of levels regarding our will. Another mentor who has helped me greatly is Kathy Kolbe, who observed that we can intend, attempt, or commit; as in intending burglary, attempting burglary, or committing burglary. Each of these carries a different level of sureness in taking action. The problem is that we often really can't make the choices we pretend we can.

I'm sure this will sound a little strange, but we aren't doing nearly the amount of choosing we like to think we do. Here is another bit of personal dishonesty. If you listen to some voices out there the self-improvement world, they make it sound like we all can just wake up in the morning and decide what is going to happen.

If we throw a few visualization vitamins in our NLP soup and heat it with massive pain and pleasure…it'll happen. Honestly, it probably won't. You can't simply get up and easily choose what you want to think, feel, and do every day. There is a little more going on than that. Remember, **the System is the Solution.**

Pretending that you can get up in the morning and simply 'choose' what you'll get accomplished is nothing short of a fantasy. You also can't wake up in the morning and decide you are gay, straight, smart, sassy, cool, stupid, beautiful, dashing, trustworthy, loyal, brave, clean, or reverent. I'm not saying your will isn't involved in all of these things, but it isn't simply a function of deciding and choosing. The will is more about coming to a conclusion, which actually shows how connected it is to both faith and reason.

In *Gone with the Wind*, Miss Scarlett holds her fist toward heaven and declares, "As God is my witness, I'll never be hungry again." She didn't go hungry again, but it wasn't because she woke up that morning in the embattled world of the former confederacy and just decided. She had a context in play and came to a conclusion that burst forth into a conviction. In this instance art put life in a frame for us. If you are of a different generation, then Neo (*The Matrix*) does the same thing when Mr. Smith and his lackeys unload their guns for the last time on Mr. Anderson. Neo simply says, "No," and the bullets stop in mid-air. Neo concluded that he was indeed 'The One', which then blossomed into a conviction of his will.

None of this says that you can't make choices, but until you can learn to be honest with yourself about what you really will choose (and won't)…well, then there isn't much of a chance of embracing *The One Success Habit.*

How Honesty Saves the Day

Imagine learning how to be so completely honest with yourself that you will know EXACTLY what you will and will not do every single day. This skill is a part of *The One Success Habit.* The most successful people you can find have mastered this habit in one way or another.

Honesty saves the day because you will quit wasting energy on trying to force yourself to do things you are not going to do. Honesty saves the day because you will quit feeling guilty about what you wanted to get done. Honesty saves the day because you will have all your energy available and focused on the actions you will take.

Have you ever carried around a secret about yourself that you were afraid would be uncovered? When it eventually came out in the open do you remember the great sense of relief you had to finally just have the truth 'out there'? Or, do you remember being in a relationship that wasn't working and wasn't going to work? Do you remember finally admitting the truth to yourself (and to the other person)? Do you recall how it allowed you to recover and focus your energy for other things that were going to work?

Honesty saves the day because your energy basically stops leaking and stops getting wasted in trying to drain the swamp you bought from Cousin Bernie. However, it isn't Bernie who has conned you into buying a snake oil remedy named False Hope; it's your real enemy, Dishonesty, who has you on the short-leash of failure.

Honesty saves the day because it will defeat the enemy of dishonesty; however, you finally must realize what you need to be honest about.

In order to succeed every day, you simply need to be honest about the only three choices you have…

Chapter 7

Three Roads Diverge:
Honesty in Your Daily Choices

Robert Frost penned now famous words when he said, "Two roads diverge in a yellow wood…" You probably have heard the rest as it describes the choice the traveler made between the more traveled and the less traveled roads. Most of us haven't noticed that Frost mentions a third road when he comments on doubting if he would "ever go back." Going back is the third road, or at least a third path, in the picture that Frost paints for the reader.

In our daily lives where **Action's the Thing**, we always have three options before us. Specifically, there is only one of three choices we can make concerning any particular action. Our honesty and dishonesty is at stake in the choice, and *The One Success Habit* is intimately connected to the choice between these three possible roads.

Putting it All Together

We are about to put together everything that we have learned so far. Just to review, here are the major points:

1. We need to define what success is for each of us.

2. Action's the Thing
3. Action is connected to Time and Change
4. Kaizen means starting with easy and constantly improving.
5. Motivation isn't just one thing; it's Here, There, Deadline, and Path.
6. If it is important it is urgent.
7. Motivation is always about the goal, the current situation, and the deadline.
8. Habits are a given and they either serve us or master us.
9. The System is the Solution
10. The #1 enemy of action is Dishonesty

All of these elements come together to help us intentionally establish *The One Success Habit.* Intentionally establishing the habit is the key. You have the ability to establish a single habit in your life that will begin to change everything because you will begin to take action. Also, let me assure you that if you find establishing this habit to be painful or frustrating, you have misunderstood something. Most likely you are leaving out one or two of the elements.

Please get ready. If I can show you how to establish a habit in a mostly pain-free way that will dramatically improve how much you get done on a daily basis, would you embrace it? Really? Would you make it happen? Awesome!

There is one more thing necessary to mention before we look at the most essential piece of the success habit you are about to create.

The Power of Today

Einstein's emphasis on relativity notwithstanding, did you know that the past and the future don't exist? I know the Sci-Fi world loves the idea that the past and the future can be happening in parallel, but you aren't going to take successful actions in the past or the future. The only place you can succeed is in the present, right now, today!

The past doesn't exist does it? I mean seriously, right now where is the past? It is in the past of course; it is no longer here. The past doesn't exist anymore therefore it doesn't exist at all.

The future doesn't exist does it? I mean seriously, right now where is the future? It is in the future of course; it isn't here yet. The future doesn't exist yet, therefore it doesn't exist at all.

Even if they do exist in the Multiverse, neither exists in a practical sense. Recognizing the fact that the past and the future do not exist in this moment really helps us to quit lying to ourselves. Lying in this way turns out to be a very dangerous practice for our success. Action can only happen in the present, in this moment, right now. There is no action you can take in the non-existent past or future; so regrets and hopes can be happily set aside.

Knowing the past and future do not exist can also make us emotionally healthier.

If you pretend the past is still around and dictating life to you, it can lead to depression. If you pretend the future is here and dictating actions to you, it can lead to anxiety. Obsessing on past regrets is depressing, while obsessing on future fears is anxiety producing. The real power is in the present…it's all that exists anyway!

The Three Roads of Honesty

There are only three possibilities when we look at something we are considering doing. You can conclude:

1. I will do it
2. I may do it
3. I will not do it

These three choices will change your life once you begin to establish the habit of total honesty regarding every action you are considering taking. In fact, this is where the problem exists for most of us. Is it where the problem has been for you?

Think about how it tends to go. You get up in the morning and make a list of things you need To Do today. You make out a long list and may even put the items in some kind of order, perhaps numbering the top six actions you want to take. Some people are more detailed and schedule work times for the items, others tend to lose the list for part of the day. It doesn't matter because almost all of us lie to ourselves to some degree or another. We are looking at a list trying to generate a commitment or obligation to get the stuff done.

The results are what you might expect. Some of it gets done and some of it doesn't.

Here lies the life changing moment for you; try honesty. Get your list out right now or make one on the spot. It needs to be a list of what you want to do today (or tomorrow if you are reading this late in the evening). After you have the list before you, just ask yourself the following question for each item:

Am I going to do this today?

Your answer can only be yes, maybe, or no. Look at each item and say aloud with honesty, "I will do this," or "I may do this," or "I will not do this."

These three roads are not about you trying, or hoping, or guilting yourself into taking action. These three choices are about being honest.

You may find that it is amazing that you can actually know if you are going to do something or not. But, think for a moment about ordinary things. Are you going to play golf with your friends Friday afternoon? As far as it depends on you, you know you will, know you may, or know you won't. How about going to Disney World this summer? What about going to the lake in July? Are you going to fix the faucet, call the client, go on a date? Every one of these can be quickly admitted to be a yes, maybe, or no.

We are not talking about a promise or a commitment. We've all had enough of trying to make ourselves to commit to something we don't care about. We are talking about a conclusion, we are admitting to ourselves what we really are (are not) committed to do. This is a special kind of awareness and honesty we all possess. It is similar the honesty we use when we admit we love (or don't love) someone.

Why is this bit of honesty so important? The answer is found in the word 'resistance'. Resistance is a force that is against another force.

Wind resistance is the force of the wind blowing against the force of a forward moving plane. A dog pulling against a leash toward another dog is resistance (or you are the resistance to the dog). Trying to get things done when there is internal resistance is challenging because part of your effort is spent on overcoming the resistance.

The three roads we have in view here present a way to remove your internal resistance almost effortlessly. Two of the choices have no resistance:

- I will
- I will not

If you are honestly going to do the thing, then there is no internal resistance. You know you are going to do it.
If you are going to the beach, or to golf, or to pay your bills, then you will. If you know you will not learn to fly, ask for a raise, or call her for a date, then you will not.

There won't be a bit of struggle or hesitation because it **is a** settled conclusion for you. The conviction is in place and your will is set. [As an aside, this doesn't mean that you can't change your mind or that something may come up to prevent taking action. It does mean that without something from the outside changing your direction, you will do it. Nothing inside of you is in the way].

Now, it is important to know that only one of the three roads has resistance naturally built into it: **I May**

If you may do something then you also may not do it. 'May' and 'may not' have forces in opposition.
It means that 'do it' is being opposed by 'don't do it' when we are in the middle spot of maybe. There is nothing wrong with 'maybe' if we are being honest about it. However, maybe is a place of being stuck between doing and not doing---the thing. We may do the thing versus we may not do the thing. Now you can understand what happens to you when you are not honest with your daily actions. If you 'try' to work on something that is a 'maybe'---you can know that there is a force working against you. Worse yet, if you 'try' to work on something you haven't honestly admitted you 'will not do'--- an even greater force is working against you.

How I Discovered the Three Roads

Please indulge me for a moment as I share with you how I discovered this life-changing insight about yes, maybe, and no.

My goal is to make this truth clearer so that you can embrace it from a deep understanding rather than from my superficial 'give it a try' explanation so far. I am naturally not a list maker; I am sporadic, loathe boredom, and tend to run five conversations at a time. What I've found is not only personal, but it is universal. There are years of reflection and study on the nature of the structures and forces that are behind the moment; but it was a series of questions I asked that brought it into the light.

A few years ago I won an award for an article I wrote for the Society of Safety Engineers (it's available for free at www.onesuccesshabit.com) on the use of questions in leadership and creativity. In the article I mention *The Better Question*. The Better Question is simply to ask a question about your question. "What's the better question?" I ask. I then answer it and ask, "Now what's the better question?"

Here are my notes as a series of questions that came about as I kept asking, "What is the better question (than I answered before)?"

.....notes.....

Observed: Some goals (etc.) I know I'll do (commitment)...[but] some goals I 'think' I'll do (no commitment)

Question: Why do I think I'll do a goal I'm not committed to?
     -because I might get committed

Q: How do we commit to a goal we aren't committed to?

Q: Is it best to only work on our commitments?

Q: How do we come to be committed to a goal?

Q: What would happen if we only worked on goals we were committed to?
    -what if we only can...?

Q: What if the ONLY categories are

Committed	or	Uncommitted?
Decided	*or*	*Undecided?*
Decided......Considering......Rejected?		
"I will"	*"I might"*	*"I won't"*
(YES)	*(MAYBE)*	*(NO)*

Q: For "To Do" – Am I going to do (work on) this or not?

Q: Is <u>urgent</u> (Time Component included in commitment) the only thing we work on?

Q: What if you can have a Goal without a Time-Frame, but you can't have Commitment without a Time Frame?
    -a Committed Goal is an Accepted Goal

*** So Commitment (may mean)
    - *The Goal is Desired / Meaningful*
    - *The Time Frame is clear (matters)*
    - *Both Pass the "I will do it" test*

.....end of notes.....

These notes are unedited and don't show all of my thinking, but they do show that wrestling with this discovery came from a struggle with the original problem of our not doing what we seem to have 'decided' to do.

What Will It Mean?

What will it mean to begin to be honest about what you will, might, and won't do? It is hard to say and you might find it a little frightening at first. What if you really don't want to do much of anything? What if there are things you finally admit you will not do…what will others think? What if you haven't decided about things you have been saying for years that you will do?

Truthfully, I don't know what it will mean. I do know that being honest will bring a new settledness into your life and a new energy to (perhaps finally) get something accomplished!

Arising every day to work on the things you honestly will work on will change your life. You will get more accomplished in a week than you used to get accomplished in a month.

If you are one of the few (like my mother who always does everything she has put on her list), then you have probably figured this out for yourself. Now you have a book to give to everyone you know that explains what you've been wanting them to 'get' for their own lives!

How to Begin

In the next chapter we are going to start building the habit. Right now all you need to do is begin to ask and honestly answer this question about any action you are thinking about taking today:

Am I going to do this today?

Next, you must look into your own heart and answer with:

1. I will
2. I may
3. I will not

Needless to say, if you are not sure then it is a definite maybe! You'll learn what to do about those 'maybes' when you answer the one burning question...

Chapter 8

What is the One Success Habit?

Hey, glad you skipped ahead to this chapter---it's where the 'meat' is for the whole book. Unfortunately I have to beg you to go back and start at the beginning. Up to this point we've looked at the foundation for the habit. If you don't really think through this foundation, then you are going to read this chapter and say, "Why?" If you will go back and read all the chapters that come before, then you will be saying, "Oh, I see!" We all walk before we run and you are holding a radical book which is built on a particular set of principles. You are a grown person so I can't make you, but PLEASE at least skim the earlier chapters before diving into this one. Thanks.

Understanding the Habit

I'm sure you've noticed by now, but I haven't actually told you what the habit is. We have looked at many things that are absolutely vital to make sense of why the habit is valuable and how we can go about building it into our lives. It is a funny thing about the 'why' and 'how' of learning anything. Most of us (Americans especially) are so busy with wanting the 'how' answered that we often completely forget the 'why' part of the story.

This lust for pragmatism is understandable, but it tempts us all to be short-termers who are just trying out a new idea. We trade the physics of success for the fads of success.

When we don't know 'why' it makes sense, we rarely have much endurance. On the other hand, we who like the 'why' of the matter will often feel like we have done all that needs doing once we understand the reasons something should work. In this mode of operation we can be busy learning, but never really acting on the information we've collected. Frankly, although **Action's the Thing**, *action with understanding* is normally a great long-term answer.

Here is *The One Success Habit (You Can't Do Without)*:

**I allow myself to get everything done
I mean to do each day.**

Please notice that this habit DOES NOT insist that you make a list every day. It's written in the present tense so you can start getting it clear in your thinking what it will feel like to have this as a firm habit in your life. It is written as you would say it to someone else. It is a habit of permission and honesty because you are taking responsibility. It has within it an established deadline of each and every day.

I can't say I learned this from my mother, but I should have. I quizzed her recently about her own 'To Do' system. She is in her mid-seventies and goes strong every single day of her life.

I asked her if she ever doesn't get her list done for the day. "Nope, never. I always get everything done every day." She is telling the truth. She has learned how to only put the things on the list that she will get done that day. In her own system, she has a different list for each day of the week and places her items according to her priorities and time. Of course, she knows what she will do on a given day. She has established the habit for herself, and among her various awards was one for *The Outstanding Young Woman of America* when she had three young children and her husband worked as an attorney and served in the Alabama Legislature. She isn't lucky, she is responsible. She wasn't visited by the gods of getting it done, she has a habit.

What would this habit mean to your life? Your story may be like mine. I have always tended to wait until the last minute, and then in a Herculean effort I'd get a shocking amount accomplished in a surprisingly short period of time. However, sometimes I'd miss and I would be stuck negotiating deadlines or turning in something of lesser quality. You may have not tried to be Hercules; maybe you have just kind of drifted on through life wanting more, but not really getting it done. You are one simple habit away from transformation.

Imagine for a moment if you had *The One Success Habit (You Can't Do Without)* automatically happening in your life each day. You would arise in the morning and, before long, re-affirm or clarify what you easily-and-without-resistance would get done that day. You would gladly get going and knock them all out, even with the interruptions and crisis-moments everyone faces.

You would no longer have guilt or frustration or frazzledness; but a happy moment with your head on the pillow, resting because you knew you had seen enough accomplished for the day. What if you knew you would get everything done you meant to get done each day? What if you could say to someone (honestly and with a straight face), **"I allow myself to get everything done I mean to do each day."**

Wait, there is a little more. How many things could you get done in a day if you had the habit and didn't fight with yourself? How many things would you get in motion if it was automatic that you get whatever you mean to get completed...completed? Two items? Five items? Ten items? Let's just hang out in the middle. You get five things you mean to get done completed each day, without having to 'make yourself' because it is automatic as a habit. What does that add up to in a month? 30 x 5 = 150, so you will be seeing 150 things completed every month that you mean to complete. Yearly, that amounts to over 1,800 items you will complete that are meaningful to you. Again, since it is a habit, it is automatic and stress-free because you won't be fighting with yourself. How in the world will you keep from succeeding with this kind of consistent action being taken? On the other hand, how can you possibly succeed if you are not putting things in motion? Remember, **Action's the Thing**; and, with 1,800 actions a year (or many more)...how do you think it is going to go?

The Habit on Two Levels

There are two levels in which *The One Success Habit* can operate.

Frankly, **Level One** is plenty, but **Level Two** is even better.

Habit Level One

Level One is the most basic place to establish the habit, and at the very least this is where you should aim. On this level you will be concerned with the decisions you face all day long. It may be a decision to drop what you are doing to help someone out, to get a part for something you are repairing, or whether or not to go out that night because of a surprise invitation. On Level One you are learning how to decide. However, it isn't how to decide that is at issue; rather it is learning to listen to what you already know. You either 'will' or you 'will not' in the moment with every decision you will ever face. If you know and admit you will, you are in a good place. If you know and admit you will not, then you are also in a good place. If you aren't sure, then you are caught in the middle of conflicting forces that will drain your time and waste your energy…and will more than likely make you wait until the last minute when someone, or something, will go ahead and decide for you. Staying in the middle with 'maybe' is where all the incompletion in action really lies.

The solution which makes up Level One is to develop the habit of asking yourself a basic question:

Will I do this?

Next, you will make it your habit to answer honestly with

1. I will
2. I may
3. I will not

Yes, that is all there is to it. As you learn to be honest you will be able to decide on the spot if you will or will not. If you are unsure, then the answer is always, "Maybe."

Here is a refinement on the questions you will find helpful. Once you have an answer of either I Will, I May, or I Will Not, ask the following:

I Will

- ✓ Will I?
- ✓ Really?
- ✓ Really?

I Will Not

- ✓ Will I not?
- ✓ Really?
- ✓ Really?

I May

- ✓ What will it take to conclude I will?
- ✓ What will it take to conclude I won't?
- ✓ Why might I?
- ✓ Why might I not?

The value of the question, "Really?" is to make it clear to yourself that you really will or really will not. If you will, then you will do it. If you will not, then you don't have to waste time or energy trying to make yourself do something you are not going to do. If you know you will do it but don't, then in forming the habit you either (a) Haven't yet learned to estimate what you can get done in a day, or (b) Are not being honest and should have said, "Maybe."

The four questions that follow "I May" help you move to the right goal for dealing with being unsure. If you answer with "I May," your goal will be to decide how you will come to conclude "I Will" or "I Will Not." Once you know what it will take to move from "I May" to "I Will / I Will Not," everything will fall into place. **This is the habit that will change everything.** Level One is simply to make this your automatic response when faced with a question about what you are going to do. Although Level One applies well to your actions in general, the practical truth that the past and the future do not exist insists that the habit is best applied to each day, which leads to…

Habit Level Two

Level Two is the most immediate and useful place to apply *The One Success Habit*. With Level Two you will be concerned with your daily 'To Do' list.

Some years ago when I was getting my certifications in a variety of personality and talents training, I was discussing what I was learning with my mother (the list maker).

She listened to the descriptions about me and we talked about what I was like as a child. At one point in the conversation she asked, "Does it say anything in there about you being a procrastinator?" Actually, it did, but I asked her instead to compare what I'd gotten accomplished to other children she had known over the years. She responded after a little reflection with a "Well, you have done a lot." I just wanted her to understand that we all can accomplish things in a variety of ways. It wasn't until my next birthday that she mentioned it again on my card. *"Dear Fred...If I had known then what I know now, I wouldn't have been so frustrated with how hard it was to potty-train you!"* Ah, a mother's love.

Whether or not you actually write down a list is not an issue, but whether or not you have a list is very much an issue. I've noticed that when things have to be done we tend to fall back on what works. Education is a good example. When education starts to fail we always go back to two things:

1. The basics of reading, writing, and arithmetic.
2. Getting a tutor (low student/teacher ratio)

If we thought clearer we would never stray from these things. The same applies to getting things accomplished on a daily basis. When we are in a crisis (or are about to go on vacation), we almost always make a list of what to do, what to pack, who to call, etc. The reason is very, very simple:

IT WORKS

Personally, my bent is to make a list and lose it, which leads to the fun of finding it later and seeing what all I got done! Most of us who loathe lists are simply under the misunderstanding that a list means slavery. It is perfectly understandable that we have this misunderstanding since we came to the conclusion by watching those of you who are enslaved to your lists!

The truth is that a list is just a tool, it's your servant. It has nothing to do with losing your ability to be spontaneous. In fact, when you determine what goes on your list by concluding I Will, I May, or I Will Not, there is no frustration at all. Your frustration comes by having things on your list without filtering them. If your list is really only about what you know you will do that day, then you've got it made in the shade; no resistance, no guilt, only steady actions that will produce the fruit you have wanted to see for years.

Even though we will look at building your system in the next chapter, you can get started right now with the following steps for a daily Will-Do list:

1. Get a 3x5 card (or larger) and divide it evenly into three columns by drawing two spaced vertical lines. Label the left column 'I will', the middle column 'I may', and the right column 'I will not'.
2. In the middle column write down everything you are hoping you MAY be able to do that day. It is really important that you only put down things you might do THAT day. This isn't a place to

gather all your To Do items for the next few weeks.

3. Now, go through the items one-by-one and ask yourself, "Am I going to do this today?" If you answer "yes or no" then ask, "Really?" a couple of times.

4. If you know in your heart you WILL do the item that day, scratch it out of the middle column and move it to the left "I Will" column.

5. If you know in your heart you WILL NOT do the item that day, scratch it out of the middle column and move it to the right "I Will Not" column.

6. Notice your list now has some items (probably) in each of the columns.

7. Now, go and do the I Will items and don't even think about the I Will Not items. The order in which you do them is almost irrelevant since you will get them all done anyway. Work on them in whatever order and whichever time of day makes sense to you.

There, that is all there is to **The One Success Habit**. If you get to some 'I May" items, then more power to you! However, as you develop the habit you will get much better at knowing what you will do that day. Of course, you will do a great deal more than is on any list because of all that comes at you in a given day. Also, sometimes emergencies will arise. So what? Here are a few final observations that are required to establish *The One Success Habit*:

- **You must honestly and truthfully sort each item.** You can't just rush through your daily list and say, "I know I'll do that one." This is not about you making a commitment, it is about knowing in your heart what you will and will not do.

- **You probably need to write down most things** that aren't 100% routine or 100% unnecessary to write down. You don't write down "take a shower," but you might write down "order copies of *The One Success Habit* for my children."

- **You really should make each item its own separate thing.** Even though you may have something to do that has many sub-points, it is a better move to list them each as their own item.

- **You want to be clear.** Write down the smaller part of a larger project you know will get done. Do not write down the project title to represent one part of the project.

- **Sometimes it may be best to precede your Will-Do item with the word 'start'.** We really can conclude that we want to work on something, but we can't quite be sure about how far we might get. One solution is just to use the word 'start' and see how it works for you. Start Reading the Marketing Book, Start Cleaning the Boat, Start a List of Possible Wedding Guests, etc. It can be an accurate Will-Do, but use it sparingly.

- **You can always ask, "What would it take for this 'I May' to become an 'I Will' (or 'I Will Not')?"**

Motivation and the Habit

We learned in Chapter 3 that motivation isn't just one thing. Moreover, we came to appreciate how there are four elements that go into motivation. *The One Success Habit (You Can't Do Without)* has the motivation built into it. Here are the three elements we discussed:

1. THERE: What you want (the goal)
2. HERE: What you have (the current situation)
3. DEADLINE: A time constraint
4. PATH: A basic idea of how you'll likely get there (or at least get started).

As you use a daily list in your Level Two approach to the habit, the goal and the current situation are clearly in mind because of the directness of the Will-Do items themselves. The list is sorted so the limits you have will also create focus (see *About Life and Uganda,* by Fred R Lybrand. Chapter 8, "Limits Yield Intensity" gives an inspiring explanation of the power of limits to create focus). Finally, the deadline is clear as a bell since it is TODAY.

Now you can really multiply the power of the habit as you realize all you have to do is…

Chapter 9

Build One of These & the Habit
Will Come Quickly

You've been misled. I'm going to have to get on a soapbox for a moment. I am about to be passionate in seeking to persuade you to change the way you think about the greatest contradiction going in the personal development literature over the decades. We've all been sold a 'bill of goods' and if we don't start to dump it right now; well, frankly, there isn't much hope for developing *The One Success Habit.*

Here's the problem, there are two messages being shared simultaneously, and often by the same speaker or writer:

> **Message 1:** "You are unique, be yourself and you will succeed."

> **Message 2:** "Imitate successful people, especially 'me' and 'my system' for (fill in the dollar amount here)."

Given that you are unique, how can you imitate successful people? Given that you are to imitate successful people, how can you be unique?

If we take these directions at face value, then we must realize they are mutually exclusive. Stop kidding yourself. Chances are deep down you've known something was amiss. We really can't do mutually exclusive things. My dad used to make this point to me in sharing how he joked with his mother when he was a teen. Every time he would leave the house my grandmother would say to him, "Bye, have fun and be good." Dad would respond with, "Now Mother, make up your mind." In other words, for a wild teen of the 1940's, being good and having fun were mutually exclusive. I'm glad times have changed…

These two messages can meet, but not the way they are expressed by the different voices out there. Consider it for a moment. Have you ever bought a 'system' and attempted to follow it exactly? How'd that work out for you? Didn't you find you tweaked it, or couldn't really follow it? Wasn't it frustrating? Now, what about the other point? Did you ever try to do things in your own totally unique way? Did you really make sense of who the 'unique you' was, and did it start producing success? In other words, how did that work out for you?

There are plenty of people who have imitated others and succeeded. And, there are plenty of people who have been uniquely themselves and succeeded. If you are among them, then congratulations! The rest of us, however, find ourselves bouncing around a lot.

Some years ago I read a study Dunn & Bradstreet had conducted on successful McDonald's franchises. They found that one group of people was more successful after buying a McDonalds than any other group. It was farmers. Yes, farmers who had sold the farm and moved to the city to run a McDonalds did better than anyone. There gave two reasons to explain the success of farmers.

1. Farmers were used to working hard.
2. Farmers knew nothing about running a restaurant or a franchise.

Hard work is obvious---it makes a big difference because **Action's the Thing**. The second point isn't so obvious. Why would ignorance be an asset? Well, it turns out that they just followed the 'McDonald's System' to the letter. They weren't smarter than all the years of research and experience McDonald's Corporate had learned. They weren't trying to improve the system (yet) or 'show them what for' by being a maverick. They just totally focused on imitation. They didn't care one whit about being unique; all they wanted was to succeed! The truth is that they worked harder AND smarter than most others.

So, are you thinking 'being unique' is a mistake? It's not a mistake at all. Do you think Steve Jobs, Bill Gates, or Jim Carrey would have succeeded by imitation? Never!

So, make a choice. Which are you? Are you an entrepreneur or a franchise owner? Neither is morally superior; in fact, neither is particularly 'sexier' than the other either.

A successful imitator outshines a failed entrepreneur. However, in time, the imitator will be a little unique as well (all McDonald's aren't exactly the same…especially the more successful ones). A successful entrepreneur also learns to do some imitating too. There is a way to balance these two orientations, and it comes down to two simple things:

Hierarchy & Principles

Hierarchy is really just about dancing. If you've ever danced (or watched it from afar) you know that one person is taking 'the lead' in the dance. The leader / follower arrangement allows the dance to flow smoothly. Imagine if neither led. Imagine if both led. In either case it would be disjointed and uncoordinated. Moreover, if you get rid of one dance partner, it changes the art from one form to another. There are four options before us when we think of being unique or imitating success. Simply put, you can be successful as one who is:

A. UNIQUE: A totally unique success
B. IMITATOR: An imitator of the successful
C. UNIQUE/Imitator: A unique person who adds in some imitation of the successful
D. IMITATOR/Unique: An imitator of the successful who adds in some uniqueness

Any of these four options will work. However, it is important for you to settle on which one you will be at heart. If you try equally to be both unique and an imitator, then you will surely bounce between the two--- attempting uniqueness and then attempting imitation.

Frankly, it will not work because you can't be both at the same time; but, being a little more one than the other really makes a big difference.

Principles are the second way you can use to overcome the confusion between uniqueness and imitation. A principle is just a bit of understanding that can be used in a variety of circumstances. In Chapter 1 we noticed that, "Principles are transferable, which means they can be applied in many settings across the boundaries of time and culture. A principle can be used in unique ways over and over again. Being principle-focused is essentially the same as being wisdom-focused." Instead of copying systems exactly, you can distill the principles involved. Instead of being perfectly unique, you can make use of the principles found in something similar to what you hope to accomplish. If you are a unique on-stage performer, you still will follow some similar moves in someone else's successful system (which honestly is still imitation). For example, you would probably have a concert tour, songs for sale online, T-shirts and CD's at the show, etc. You would be following a pattern, but you would still be different enough to be called unique.

Using Your Personality

> *Whatever you are by nature, keep to it; never desert your own line of talent. Be what nature intended you for and you will succeed; be anything else and you will be ten thousand times worse than nothing.*
>
> - Sydney Smith

Your personality is a set of traits that help you operate as a unique individual. Whether it is genetic or learned (the studies say it is clearly both), honoring your personality is what will make the difference between success and failure. You may be more prone to following a system (imitation) or creating your own system from scratch (unique), but understand that either one can serve you well. Blake made an observation that perfectly underscores the point:

> *I must create a system or be enslaved by another man's.*
>
> -William Blake

If you are going to develop *The One Success Habit*, then you will need to develop a system or follow someone else's. There are plenty of people you know who have mastered this habit; but, if you try to build the habit the way they do it, you will likely fail miserably. Why would you fail? Simply put, it is because you have a unique personality (even if you prefer to imitate successful people). It still must be a system you follow that will work for you. There are some extreme exceptions; for example, the military seems to know how to get everyone to conform to a system for cleaning a rifle (or cleaning a sleeping area). The military takes away choice for a while. But, if you are going to grow the habit, you will need to make good use of your ability to choose.

Many Systems, One Result

The point in all of this is that you need to clearly recognize two things:

1. You must use a system to build the habit.
2. Which system you use probably won't matter much as long as it is your own system or a system that matches your nature.

Most of us made it through high school and completed the infamous 'term paper' didn't we? You may not know this, but most of us also made similar grades. Some grades were higher while some grades were lower; but, we all got it done. Did we do it the same way? No we did not. Some of us had lots of help. Some of us started early and worked steadily. Others still, started late and worked furiously. The point here is that the exact process often doesn't matter, so long as the result is what you wanted.

If you are going to develop
***The One Success Habit (You Can't Do Without)*,**
**then all that finally matters is IF you build the habit,
not HOW you build it.**

Said differently, if you don't develop the habit, your system didn't work.

How to Build Your System

To "build your system---build your habit," you need to simply employ a couple of things we've discussed throughout the book:

1. A Procedure
2. Kaizen

Sam Carpenter's book, *Work the System*, gives us a nice way to approach building a system. He explains that a set of steps in order (a procedure) helps establish a system. That really is how it works with everything from Walt Disney World to wakeboarding.

In particular, Mr. Carpenter suggests using three elements:

✓ The Objective
✓ The Guidelines / Principles
✓ The Steps

He insists that this is to be written down so it is very clear to all involved; in this case, you alone. He is right. You really must write it down. The objective is simply what you want:

**As a habit, I allow myself to get everything
done I mean to do each day.**

The guidelines would be any helpful thoughts you might like to list such as;

Action's the Thing
What I do daily = what I did for a lifetime
I reap as I sow
Habits are servants

The procedure is the steps you will follow. An example might be:

1. When I sit down every morning in my chair, I take a 3x5 card and list all I hope to do that day in a middle column (or perhaps you make this list at night).
2. I sort my list by looking at each item and carefully asking myself, "Will I do this today?" I then ask, "Really?" And again, "Really?"
3. I move the items 'I will do' into the left column and the items 'I will not do' into the right column (while scratching them out of the middle column).
4. I number the left (will do) column in the order I want to do them. The order doesn't much matter because I 'will do' them all.
5. I set a time to start on the first 'will do' item.
6. If I have time left over after completing my 'will do' items, I'll consider working on something in the middle (maybe) column. But, more than likely I'll just celebrate!

Now that you can see how a procedure should look, adding Kaizen will make your success inevitable. Kaizen means that you want to seek to constantly improve your procedure for establishing your habit. Three Kaizen questions are really all you need:

1. Is my procedure easy enough for me to do?
2. Is my procedure getting me the result I want?
3. How could I make it a little bit better?

Remember, all you want the procedure to do is to establish a habit. As you begin to use your procedure you may find it is too hard to work on at night, so you change that step (or the other way around). You may find that having the 'maybe column' as a possibility distracts you---so you move all your 'maybe items' to the 'will not do' list. As you work with the procedure you will find ways to make it better for you personally. You may even create steps that involve your phone or your computer. Other steps may involve showing what you accomplished to your spouse or a mentor. It really is about you establishing a starter procedure and improving it as you need to...until *The One Success Habit* is automatic. Will it take twenty-one days? Who knows? The key is to simply do it every day until you don't think about it anymore because you just do it without thought, or willpower, or struggle. Then, and only then, is it your servant. Of course, questioning your procedure on a daily basis would be like checking your pulse every five minutes. Try your procedure for a week or two, then tweak it as you can.

As you work with your own system for establishing the habit, you will probably experience the kinds of things I did.

- ➤ Sometimes I failed because I wasn't honest and slipped into trying to make myself do a few 'maybe' items.
- ➤ Sometimes I would just put one thing on the list for the day (which really was pretty cool if it was that important a priority).
- ➤ Sometimes I would change up the expected order because circumstances changed.
- ➤ Sometimes a crisis took over and I had to have a 'better luck tomorrow' approach. Of course, I do

mean to take care of every true crisis when it happens, so my *One Success Habit* is working.

You will find that you are going to be on your own path, but you will get there if you make the procedure easy enough and don't allow exceptions. Exceptions throw habits aside. Even on vacation it is best to follow your procedure to the letter. On vacation, however, your 'Will-Do' list should have things about relaxing, taking a nap, basking in the sun, hiking the trail, smiling more at your family, etc. Even on vacation you mean to do something, even if it is nothing at all!

The Point of Decision

Where are you now? Have you come to a conclusion that you will develop *The One Success Habit (You Can't Do Without)*? Really? No, really? Remember, your options are only three-fold:

1. I **will** develop *The One Success Habit*
2. I **may** develop *The One Success Habit*
3. I **will not** develop *The One Success Habit*

If you know in your heart you will develop *The One Success Habit*, then go for it and see what 1,800 actions will mean to your next year. If you will not, thanks for your honesty. If you only 'may' develop *The One Success Habit*, then ask yourself the questions we looked at earlier:

✓ What will it take to conclude I will develop *The One Success Habit?*

- ✓ What will it take to conclude I won't develop *The One Success Habit?*
- ✓ Why might I develop *The One Success Habit?*
- ✓ Why might I not develop *The One Success Habit?*

Once you conclude you will make *The One Success Habit* your own, build a procedure you will find easy to do, even if it means only having one 'I will' conquered a day at first.

What if we really are responsible for everything that happens to us?

You can see your life dramatically change with more ease than you ever imagined if you will build *The One Success Habit (You Can't DO Without)* into your daily life. Also, the word 'Do' is a placeholder word for taking action. We have been talking about the one habit that matters in all the 'doing' in life. We can easily adapt it to your job or hobby or dream:

- *The One Success Habit* You Can't **Sell** Without
- *The One Success Habit* You Can't **Write** Without
- *The One Success Habit* You Can't **Study** Without
- *The One Success Habit* You Can't **Build** Without
- *The One Success Habit* You Can't **Lead** Without

Now, any final confusion about *The One Success Habit* usually comes down to this question…

Chapter 10

What about Goals, Projects, and Teams?

An expert is a man who tells you a simple thing in a confused way in such a fashion as to make you think the confusion is your own fault.

-Aldous Huxley

If you are confused it is because Huxley was right, you didn't read the book, or there are some lingering questions. *The One Success Habit (You Can't Do Without)* is an approach specifically geared to you as an individual. Our individual lives, however, aren't simply organized around the basics of each day. Personal goals and the interactions with others inform a great deal of what we face every day at home, at the office, and in our charitable efforts. And yet, if we don't master the daily habit of doing what we mean to do each day, then what does the rest of it matter?

In this book you are following a basic pattern for transformation that is as ancient as the faintest ink on the driest parchment from history. Better thinking leads to better actions leads to better results. It amounts to this phrase---

First Understand, then Underway

It means that we want to think in a clear way about strategic matters before we rush off into action. Though **Action's the Thing**, the way we think informs the kind of actions we will take (or avoid). Even if you have great instincts, you must learn to think "trust them." This book has been about inviting you to think in a very fresh way as the basis for taking some very fresh actions…all on the way to establishing a life-transforming habit. What might be lingering in your thinking is how this applies to other important aspects of our lives. So, briefly, let's think about goals, projects, and teams.

Goals

In Chapter 2 we stated,

> *A goal is simply an end result that you want to see happen. A goal can be a fine meal, an original work of art, or improved sales for a product. A goal is simply what you are aiming at; although we can call it a target, objective, creation, event, result, or outcome.*

Goals and daily Will-Do's are essentially the same, the difference is only the size of the objective; or more accurately, how far out in time you mean for it to take to complete. There also is an important difference in that Will-Do's are things you can control, while what we mean by 'goals' is sometimes better called 'wishes' or 'wants' to be precise.

Goals can be defined by when they are due (weekly, monthly, yearly) or by what they are (finish college, get married, climb Kilimanjaro, etc.). Ultimately, there is a day that comes when the completion of the goal is merely the last Will-Do in a long chain of actions. While goal setting is very important, you can see that *The One Success Habit* is absolutely essential.

Projects

A project is also a kind of goal, however the emphasis with a project is having all the steps (sub-goals) organized and coordinated to reach an outcome. A project emphasizes the carefully thought-through nature of an outcome which requires a more complex approach to planning. Projects also normally involve a number of different players who are making separate contributions to the final outcome. In organizations and businesses, projects normally require both oversight and hierarchy; which simply means there are a number of individuals, suppliers, vendors, and sub-contractors who are doing the job they signed on to do.

Teams

Teams are currently the most misunderstood and mis-defined part of the business and organizational world. Everything is done by 'teams' these days, and everyone is on the team.

A team, however, isn't merely a group of people in some way connected to an outcome. If this were the case, my Alabama Crimson Tide could not pull off a single victory without me (I assure you they do win without me...I don't even think positive thoughts all the time!). Well, teams can have slackers and detractors and still get the job done, but you get the point.

A team is actually a group of people whose interaction is necessary to accomplish a mutually understood end result. I'm sure there are fancier definitions, but none are more practical. In general, each person is vital to the outcome; which means that each person has a voice in what is happening. Some voices carry less weight, but they still matter on a true team. Most of us don't know how the little bits of feedback from the linemen can influence the quarterback or the coach's decisions. Projects are more like a factory or an assembly line, while teams are more like a family with older children who are still at home. All we really need to have in our bag of tools is...

The Three Answers

The Three Answers are the essentials necessary to keep in mind when we consider the application of *The One Success Habit* to goals, projects, and teams. The three answers are **Time**, **Professionalism**, and **Cooperation**.

Time

In Chapter 3 we learned about time as the third element of what ultimately generates motivation. When you think of *The One Success Habit* for your daily life or your organization, the time element is already established. A Will-Do list is for that day (or perhaps a week). You may define the day by quitting time, bedtime, or some other set measure; but, it still has the limit of the day.

Goals, projects, and teams naturally do not have such a consistent and clear-cut deadline. Each situation is different and is influenced by a variety of factors. Finally though, someone(s) decides the deadline for completion. This deadline then serves to help organize the various steps involved in a goal, a project, or a team effort.

So, how does this relate to *The One Success Habit*? It is simple:

You or your project or your team must still be subject to *I Will*, *I May*, or *I Will Not*

No matter your role or the roles of others, it still comes down to a daily effort based on answering the question, "Will I (or we) work on _____ today (this week, month, year, etc.)?" You either know you will, know you may, or know you will not. Both our rational mind and intuition can cooperate here for your knowing.

It is a very powerful exercise for team members to have an honest conversation about this question concerning the various goals they are working on together.

It is also a very powerful conversation you can have with yourself about your own larger goals or project objectives. Am I going to have a pool installed in the backyard this summer? Really? Really? Am I going to finish this report by Friday at noon? Really? Really?

As we've learned, understanding that you 'may' reach a deadline allows you to ask a different set of questions along the lines of, "What will it take for me to decide I will or I will not reach the deadline?" Also, concluding you will not reach the deadline allows you to make a number of strategic decisions while you still have time to work with the situation. How many people are derailed by pretending? Remember, dishonesty is the #1 enemy of action.

Professionalism

Professionalism has fallen on hard times, which is great news for your career if you act like a professional. The virus weakening professionalism is something very popular these days called "buy in." Professionalism means that you do a job you've agreed to do because you have agreed to do it. A professional doesn't spend a lot of time obsessing on feelings or fairness. A professional knows that fairness is found in her decision to accept the job, and in her freedom to quit and pursue a different job.

Buy-in is a different animal altogether. Well meant, and very appropriate at times, buy in elevates everyone's opinion to an equal status.

Buy-in is focused on everyone coming to agreement and can carry a rather unprofessional attitude of, "I didn't agree so I'm not doing it." While buy-in makes sense on an initial change in direction for a business, company, or department, it loses its glitter when reality is considered. Even if a business gets 'buy-in' initially, what happens when new people are hired? Does the company start all over and get everyone's buy-in again? Of course not! After you get buy-in, you want to hire professionals who will do their jobs. You want to hire individuals who understand what they have signed on to do in their day-to-day work.

Professionalism is important with both projects and teams, but especially with projects where you have little say once you are hired to do a particular job. Why not smile and do what you were hired to do? "But it's wrong / foolish / less efficient / not up to code," you say. OK, share your concerns, but after that be a professional---work or quit.

Try asking yourself the question, "Am I going to do the job I've been hired to do?" The answer will be, "I Will, I May, or I Will Not." You know what to do from here, don't you?

Cooperation

Perhaps this goes without saying, but team members really must cooperate to accomplish together. In a way we might call this "professionalism in relationships." Sometimes the pettiness of people who are working together is astounding.

In my Theta Chi fraternity days at the University of Alabama, Bill and I didn't really see eye-to-eye, and not because he was seven inches taller. Bill was a leader and I was a leader, but we were trying to share the same mountain (the pledge class). The cure was to make us scrub the East Wing bathroom at the fraternity house until we were better. Fortunately neither of us liked cleaning, so we came to an agreement and united around the one thing we had in common--- staying out of trouble as long as we were pledges.

Really, that is the key. Most team members don't need marriage counseling, they just need to keep their eyes on the objective and their focus on today. When a team can clearly define the result they want together and unite by answering the question, "Are we going to accomplish this goal together?" then all is calm, all is bright. I'm not being sacrilegious, I'm being obvious.

Even a quick study of the great leaders and great movements will show that people unite best around a single objective. Just think about the birth of nations, civil rights, and Apple Computer.

On a far more mundane scale, when a team can define its aim clearly together and add, "What deadline can we agree to commit to for this goal?" From this moment *The One Success Habit* helps everyone start focusing on the doing and not on the frustrations with one another.

Enough said.

Appendix A

The May-Do Catalog

There is an outstanding chance that the following ideas will be the most valuable things I offer you. Many people won't read them, so all the advantage is to you right now.

Please recall that my passion is to simply---

Help you think better
to
Help you choose better actions
to
Help you get better results

When I get hired to help any person's business, or organization, they all find that I guarantee this exact sequence for any challenge they face.

We all need to re-think goals and our daily To-Do's. There is a myth out there that is all-but-an-assumption about life and how it works.

There is hardly anything that distracts you more than this assumption. Simply put, almost everyone assumes that what you want already exists deep within…and your purpose in life is to find that want and fulfill it. This notion is nothing short of magnificent baloney! Here's the truth:

You Can't Want IT
Before You Know About IT

There is not a mysterious desire mechanism in human beings; indeed, I prophesy they will never figure out exactly why any one person wants any one thing. Robert Fritz puts it right when he says, "You want what you want and you don't want what you don't want." Whether you imagine a desired something yourself or see it somewhere else is irrelevant. Wanting is unique to you, but it always follows knowing about the thing first.

You may want to eat, but you will never honestly say that you want-and-only-want Bill Bayley's West Indies Salad in Mobile, Alabama, unless you know about it. Desires work this way. Seriously, can you think of a single thing you've ever wanted apart from being able to identify it? Really? How do you know? However, once you know about Bill Bayley's unique crab salad you may just make the trip to get what you want.

The Analogy: A Catalog

Think about catalogs you enjoy. I'm fond of gadgets and clever devices.

I can look through these catalogs and suddenly declare, "I didn't know they made that…I want one!" I remember when we had an incredibly small backyard and two large dogs. I found a 'doggie septic system' that allowed us to put their deposits in the ground to be 'disposed of' by entirely natural (and non-offensive) processes. It was so cool. We wouldn't have to bag it and take it out to the dumpster. I wanted it and I got it! Did I have a predisposed want for a doggie septic tank? Not a chance. I wanted it AFTER I had the thought of it.

All of your typical daily To-Do items and goals work the same way as you develop *The One Success Habit (You Can't Do Without)*:

**I allow myself to get everything done
I mean to do each day.**

Steve Jobs thought about it this way, "People don't know what they want until you show them." Henry Ford said, "If I had asked people what they wanted, they would have said faster horses."

No one is preprogrammed with what they want to do each day. The winds of change and the choices within contribute to our desires. And yet, there is a mystical aspect to desire…sometimes it can be clarified as sin, but sometimes it is surely the Spirit moving us. This mystery allows us to play a far more honest game once we admit it.

We are both rational and intuitive. We are also both base and noble. You are not required to follow any desire, even if it is your passion.

You have the opportunity to come to a conclusion, to exercise faith, even in your day-to-day adventure labeled, "Life."

Personally, my own system replaces the To-Do List with a Will-Do List. But, you might like reframing your To-Do's as items in a catalog that you can rummage through to pick and choose according to your whims, priorities, and the voices of those you trust nearby. Here is how you can start:

The Process:

1. Instead of a Master To-Do list, establish a Master May-Do Catalog.
2. Organize this catalog according to specific categories and goals you have. The easiest form is to list things you'd like to be, do, and have.
3. Place all the To-Do's that come across your path in each of the categories or under the goals you have in mind to pursue.
4. Survey this catalog on a daily (or weekly) basis as it fits your own system. Please see Chapter 9 for details on how to build your system.
5. As an item is accomplished in your Master May-Do Catalog, scratch it through or check it off.
6. Update your catalog by creating a new catalog; carefully transferring items that are not yet completed (or removed because "I Will Not" prevailed) to the updated Catalog.

These are the basics as you build your own system. You have a 'catalog mentality' that collects things you 'may do' in the course of time. The May-Do Catalog serves as a collection of possibilities you can 'shop' through on a regular basis.

Common areas you may consider: Family, Friendships, Making Money, Health, Hobbies, Work, Learning, Recreation, Finances, and Spiritual Life.

Common goals to consider: No goal is really common…it is unique to you.

Appendix B

Buffer Days

Dan Sullivan and The Strategic Coach first introduced me to the idea of a 'Buffer Day', so all kudos to our Canadian friends!

A Buffer Day is nothing more than a day to clean up messes and get organized. It is truly one of those ideas that is so apparent that it doesn't seem special. However, just think about it. Taking a day to simply clean up messes really allows you to generate a great deal of focus on other days.

We all know it is true; being productive creates things that need cleaning up. Most of us ignore the need to reorganize and clean up until we are simply overwhelmed. A Buffer Day is far more strategic when it is chosen rather than forced upon us.

Imagine setting aside a day when your only "I Will" is to clean up all the messes you can. These days might focus on organizing folders, or returning calls, or answering email. The day could also simply involve meeting with the various members of your team or staff to let them get you caught up on everything that is going on in their own areas.

It could also give them the opportunity to ask questions they need answered in order to move ahead. Instead of seeing all of this as an interruption, you could simply have as your "I Will" for the day to be this sort of important focus.

Don't underestimate Dan Sullivan's insight. A Buffer Day sets you up for incredible productivity on another day---undistracted by the messes you have cleaned away to your own benefit.

Indeed, a solid Buffer Day is almost a prerequisite to...

Appendix C

Edison Days

The story is told that Thomas Alva Edison, the great genius who gave us the phonograph, the commercially viable light bulb, and the mechanism for electricity in every home and business (along with a total of 1093 patents), was asked by a reporter to explain his prolific life. Edison simply observed that everyone has the same sixteen waking hours in a day. He went on to explain that where most people focus on a number of things in a day, he only focused on one.

Could it really be that simple? Could it be that a single-minded focus can produce that kind of contribution and wealth through a single human being? Well, you figure it out.

I do know that when I personally have something really important to me (especially my taxes), I totally focus on the goal at hand by REFUSING to work on anything else.

Why not occasionally try Edison's wisdom and have and Edison Day? In other words, why not have a single day where you have one-and-only-one thing to accomplish on your Will-Do list?

If you get other things done too, well then Hallelujah!

Try an Edison Day; a day where you only have one thing that you know you will accomplish that day. It's probably good if it is important, but nonetheless, it still is the only "I Will" on your list. This kind of focus is, in many ways, the ultimate way to focus on anything. What's the harm of giving one day to the experiment? You might just have a genius inside of you waiting for that kind of focus.

> ***If we did all the things we are capable of, we would literally astound ourselves.***

> -Thomas A. Edison

Appendix D

The Will-Do Master List System

Some years ago, while consulting for Pioneer Natural Resources, I was included in a high-powered satellite linked training with the likes of Steven Covey, Peter Senge, Tom Peters, and a host of other stars of the day. We met in a movie theatre for the training monthly for three sessions. This was happening all over the country with some audiences having 'voting machines' for real-time feedback. In the very last session, Steven Covey polled the voters about how consistently they had used his time management system included with our training. While the votes were being uploaded and tabulated, I turned to one of the executives I was sitting with and said, "Thirty-three percent." In a few moments, and with great dismay, Covey announced that only thirty-five percent had used the system consistently.

I'm not a prophet. I just followed a bell curve. I know I couldn't use his system because I don't have a Steven-Covey-like personality. In fact, that is the problem we face in managing time---we are all different. In particular, very few of us (I'd say about thirty-three percent) have the energy to regiment ourselves. Of course, we can all do it in the military or under other types of duress, but when the pressure is gone, then so is our time management.

In over forty years of trying to figure out how to be more productive while still resembling a human being, I have not found a system that works more effectively for everyone than the basics of what I am about to show you here. A complete course with detailed training is available at www.onesuccesshabit.com. Nonetheless, you will have plenty to work with if you'll try the basic principles I outline here.

The Basics: The Will-Do List & a Calendar

Practically speaking, your daily time is either Fixed or Unfixed. Fixed time is when we have an appointment to be with someone or to do something. This time can be formally fixed on a calendar or informally fixed in our heads (check email before leaving the office). The un-fixed time is the larger blocks of time in which we don't have specific commitments, but rather make choices about what we will focus our energy upon next. Fixed time makes use of a Calendar. Unfixed time makes use of the Will-Do List.

The Will-Do Master List is the essential ingredient of this system. I like paper, so I use journals to make my own list. There is no numbering or prioritizing, just an ongoing list of all the things you will do. This is not a To-Do List or a May-Do List; it is only for those actions you will do. Specifically, you are asking and answering our questions which make up the Will-Do Test, **"Will I do this? Really? Really?"**

I'm not sure why anyone would ever want another kind of list.

Most To-Do lists just create a long chain of disappointment, guilt, and undue pressure. Let's call this To-Do Voodoo, since it really has the final effect of cursing those who dabble in it. The sense of progress is doomed for most who simply keep a running tab of all the things possible to them. Personally, I no longer have To-Do or May-Do lists anywhere; why would I need them anyway? I do keep a separate journal for my goal planning and my May-Do Catalog (see Appendix A), which includes larger results I am considering pursuing. My true commitments are only on my own Master Will-Do List and my calendar---that's it.

A calendar is the second element in the system. I use an online calendar that stays in the cloud, but if you like paper, great. Your calendar is actually just another Will-Do List, but it's one that is organized according to a place-holder in time. Basically, when you put something on your calendar, don't you normally mean that it is a commitment? Sometimes it is not set, so we 'pencil it in' or add a question mark to the event until it is confirmed. Nonetheless, you want to develop the habit of placing items on a calendar (even if it is only a mental calendar) that are also filtered by asking our questions, "Will I do this? Really? Really?" If you put something you will attend or work on during a specific time slot, then there is no need to put it on your Will-Do List.

How It Works: The Power of a Closed List

To give credit where it is due, I want to offer a shout out to Mark Forster, a UK time management consultant who has a very helpful understanding of time and accomplishment.

Although it was in 2010 when I wrote the first draft of *The One Success Habit* and developed the idea of a Will-Do List in my own labors, Mark Forester had much the same notion and wrote about it in his work, *Do It Tomorrow and Other Secrets of Time Management*, which I only recently discovered. Forster points out that a Will-Do List is a closed list that includes only those items you are committed to do. Closed lists are clearly more useful as they generate focus through the power of limits. Also, the order in which you do the items on any closed list is rarely that important (since you will do them all anyway). In *Rework*, Fried and Hansson also aim toward the power of a closed list with their observation that "Long lists don't get done." Their recommendation is to shorten a long To-Do list into lots of small To-Do lists. While helpful, this still isn't quite there since they are still wrestling with To-Do Voodoo.

Finally, as I have worked through the issue from a systems perspective, there is also no resistance on this list; the Will-Do List is only made up of those things you know you will do. Every 'maybe' means there is built-in resistance in terms of reasons for and reasons against.

The Basics of Using a Will-Do List

Again, we have a complete training to help you design your very own unique time management system (www.onesuccesshabit.com), however the following is plenty to get started:

1. The only system that will work for you is your system---so build it.

2. Keep everything you know you will do (No, Maybe, or Won't-Do items) on one Will-Do List.

3. Daily create a Focus List by pulling out the next items from your Will-Do List that you know you will do that day. This list can be re-loaded several times as you are learning how much you really can get done in a day.

4. On balance, contrary to lots of opinions, you'll probably plan your day itself most effectively at the beginning in the morning. The reason is simple; you will have a better combination of your reasoning and intuitive decision making processes. You will also have a clearer sense of the energy you have for the day.

5. Larger projects deserve their own separate Will-Do List.

6. Keep learning what works for you and improve it.

7. Use your Calendar as your other Focus List of things you will do by appointments.

8. Follow your system every day until it is a habit.

9. Follow your system every day because it is a habit – *The One Success Habit*

Additional Resources

www.ONEsuccessHABIT.com

Free Workbook for *The One Success Habit*

Free resources and personalized training to develop *The One Success Habit* (*You Can't Do Without*) is also available. A free workbook and other companion material are available at www.onesuccesshabit.com for anyone who wants to systematically work on developing *The One Success Habit.*

Sam Carpenter – A practical entrepreneur who explains the systems approach to everyday issues in life and business in his book, *Work the System.* (www.workthesystem.com)

Mark Forster – Time management philosopher and consultant who authored *Do It Tomorrow and Other Secrets of Time Management.* (www.markforster.net)

Robert Fritz – Robert is easily the greatest promoter of the creative process alive today. You are already behind if you haven't read all of Robert Fritz's works. Even if you find yourself disagreeing with Robert, you will be better off for the disagreement. In my experience, you create even better results once you understand Robert's work. (www.robertfritz.com)

Eli Goldratt – The genius behind constraints theory. Start by reading his book, *The Goal.* (www.goldratt.com)

Kathy Kolbe – Creator of the Kolbe Conative Index which shows your unique design for success. (www.kolbe.com)

Rich Schefren – Online business maven and coach (www.strategicprofits.com)

Peter Senge – Author of the classic systems thinking book, *The Fifth Discipline.* (www.solonline.org)

Dan Sullivan – The classically educated originator of The Strategic Coach (www.strategiccoach.com)

Contact Info:

Dr. Fred Ray Lybrand
fredraylybrand@onesuccesshabit.com

www.onesuccesshabit.com
www.fredraylybrand.com
www.trimtabsolutions.com

About the Author

Fred Ray Lybrand is a father of five who has been married for over 30 years and has the diverse combination of formally studying law, communication, systems thinking, linguistics, writing, theology, marketing, structural dynamics, leadership/management, and human personality. As the author of six books and a number of articles, the co-founder of TrimTab Solutions (an Energy Industry consulting firm), and The Writing Course, Dr. Lybrand is currently focusing on the challenging puzzle of human productivity and high performance. The ONE SUCCESS HABIT is his newest contribution to help individuals and organizations become more productive without yielding one ounce of being human. His client list includes the United States Air Force, State Farm Insurance, Valero, Chick-fil-A, Pioneer Natural Resources, Encana, Marathon Oil, Rose & Associates, Protrader, Burlington Resources, AcuFocus, and Silver Creek Oil & Gas.

Fred's systems perspective and keen ability to simply summarize complexity helped the AcuFocus Executive team craft a solid 18 month operating plan that has resulted in a better way of working for the entire company. We are in a better place because of our involvement with Fred Ray Lybrand.

- Dan Siems, COO, AcuFocus, Inc.

www.ingramcontent.com/pod-product-compliance
Lightning Source LLC
Chambersburg PA
CBHW051321170526
45166CB00002B/640